About the Author

Helen Fein studied at Brooklyn College and Columbia University, receiving her Ph.D. in sociology in 1971 from Columbia. As a sociologist, her work has been concerned primarily with collective violence and genocide. In this book, Dr. Fein expands some insights gleaned from her book, *Accounting for Genocide: National Responses and Jewish Victimization during the Holocaust,* winner of the 1979 Sorokin Award of the American Sociological Association "for a brilliantly original interpretation of a complex and singular historical process, that has until now defied comprehensive social analysis." The author views the sociological imagination as a lens through which one may see how good and evil emerge from social action. During 1979–80, she helped to organize New Paltz Citizens Concerned About Indochinese Refugees (CAIR) and served as its president. Her experiences in that role led her to this study. Dr. Fein lives with her husband, Richard J. Fein, in New Paltz, New York.

T5-BCI-526

Congregational Sponsors of Indochinese Refugees in the United States, 1979–1981

Congregational Sponsors of Indochinese Refugees in the United States, 1979–1981

Helping beyond Borders

Helen Fein

Rutherford ● Madison ● Teaneck
Fairleigh Dickinson University Press
London and Toronto: Associated University Presses

© 1987 by Helen Fein

Associated University Presses
440 Forsgate Drive
Cranbury, NJ 08512

Associated University Presses
25 Sicilian Avenue
London WC1A 2QH, England

Associated University Presses
2133 Royal Windsor Drive
Unit 1
Mississauga, Ontario
Canada L5J 1K5

The paper used in this publication meets the requirements
of the American National Standard for Permanence of Paper
for Printed Library Materials Z39.48-1984.

Library of Congress Cataloging-in-Publication Data

Fein, Helen, 1934–
    Congregational sponsors of Indochinese refugees
in the United States, 1979–1981.

    Bibliography: p.
    Includes index.
    1. Church work with refugees—United States.
2. Refugees—Asia, Southeastern.   3. Refugees—United
States.   4. Interdenominational cooperation.
5. Altruism—Case studies.   I. Title.
HV645.F45   1987   362.8'7   85-45952
ISBN 0-8386-3279-3 (alk. paper)

Printed in the United States of America

To the memory of
Robert E. Meyer
1928–1981

Contents

Preface

This book presents a study of congregations sponsoring Indochinese refugees in one American county between 1979 and 1981 and seeks to answer the question of how, why, and when people help members of other groups to whom they owe no obligation, which may be called collective altruism. Since the question of whether bystanders will be hostile, indifferent, or helpful is critical for lifesaving, this has determined to a significant extent the outcome of the major crises of our time.

My concern and professional interest in this question have consistently interacted and reinforced each other. I was drawn to organizing sponsorship of the Indochinese refugees in 1979 because it seemed to me that the opportunity to save them was a test case of the readiness of western states to tolerate a latent genocide similar to the way the west was tested in 1938 by the Jewish refugee crisis prefacing the Holocaust. Because I had spent five years working on research that assessed the impact of state cooperation or resistance to Nazi plans to decimate the Jews (*Accounting for Genocide: National Responses and Jewish Victimization during the Holocaust [1979]*), I was convinced of the importance of immediate and organized response to threats against minorities. *Accounting for Genocide* fortified the evidence that it was the indifference or complicity of critical bystanders and of the Allies that most directly accounted for (along with the timing and strategy of the SS) most of the differences in the proportion of Jews caught in different nations. Where widespread social defense of the Jews was organized promptly, commanding the allegiances and support of critical organizations and actors, the majority of Jews were saved. The most critical actor (apart from the state itself) was the dominant church. For this reason, I saw the churches and voluntary organizations as critical actors in organizing American support to provide temporary havens in Asia and to establish new homes for the boat people and other Indochinese refugees during the 1979 crisis. I began talking about the need to respond to Vietnam's drive to expel the boat people—leading many to watery graves and death, robbery and rape by pirates—during interviews for *Accounting for Genocide,* and I began inquiries to learn how community groups, congregations, and individuals could sponsor the refugees.

This led to my organizing and leading a community-wide interfaith sponsorship group (not included in this study) and my appointment as director of an "Indochinese refugee sponsorship development project," which was initiated by an interfaith council in another county in 1979–80; the project was to end in twelve months. Because of this role, I was more likely to be seen by the people interviewed for this study as an activist, a coparticipant and leader in the movement—and in some cases, a confidante or friend—than as a social scientist.

Yet in one sense I was still an outsider while an insider to the movement. I lived outside the county and had had little prior experience of congregational life—especially church life—at that time. As a Jew and representative of an interfaith council, I preferred to conceive of moral obligation within a Judeo-Christian framework rather than through the Christological vision that moved some sponsors. My role has been made as explicit as possible in chapters 3 and 4 so that the readers may infer what influence it might have had on the processes of commitment and the development of sponsorship.

As a participant-observer, I experienced and could appreciate the feelings of sponsorship leaders with whom I was in daily contact for a year: their enthusiasm and their exasperation—with officials, with the voluntary organizations through which they sponsored, with other group members, and at times with the refugees themselves. I could also appreciate the constant drain on the time of a few in each group, a contribution unlikely to be reported in the press. What most recall without suppressing recognition of the problems is the enduring and unexpected positive consequences for them: their exhilaration on the refugees' arrival, the lasting reciprocal affection, and their pride in giving the refugees a new start personally. "We got more than we gave them" is an often-repeated comment, summing up the feelings of sponsors. Little of this was reported in the press, which usually cited refugees and problems together: ethnic tensions, racist violence, discrimination, unemployment, and dependency. Because the focus was on the refugees, there was little public awareness of the breadth of the sponsorship movement.

After the year that the sponsorship project was completed, I initiated this study in order to understand how this movement caught on, how helping refugees became the norm in their churches and in the county, what distinguished the leaders, and how the sponsorships themselves evolved. Although helping behavior has become a critical question in social psychology in the last decade, there has scarcely been any sociological attention paid to groups or collectivities helping others, other than the self-help movement. Economic and sociobiological models of social life that have been popularized view ethnocentrism and preference for one's own kind as natural, presenting no explanation of why groups might help members of other groups or collectivities. Empirically, we also lack studies of helping by groups, movements, or networks; virtually all studies of helping behavior are of individuals making independent decisions. Chapter 1 considers the state of theory and reviews what we know about the helping behavior of individuals. Chapter 2 infers the preconditions for successful lifesaving from studies of social defense of Jews during the Holocaust. The preconditions inferred from this evidence are related to social psychological studies of helping behavior and identification with victims to devise the model proposed in chapter 3.

Chapter 2 also considers how collective memories of our national failure to anticipate, deter, or counteract the annihilation of European Jewry organized by Nazi Germany—to take in refugees, to organize rescue and give any resources to lifesaving—affected the perception of the Indochinese crisis of 1978–79 by national and religious leaders. The model of commitment and mobilization of helping proposed is illustrated in chapter 3, showing how well it conforms to the sample of sponsorships studied in Riverside County (pseudonym). The impact of collective helpfulness is assessed in chapter 4, which also explores the adaptation of refugees, the social career of refugee committees as sponsors, the refugee-sponsor bond, and the costs and rewards of sponsorship. Chapter 5 sums up my conclusions on what congregational sponsorship of refugees reveals about collective altruism and its implications for refugee policy, viewing congregational sponsorship as one model for the resocialization of refugees and immigrants that may be compared with governmental and other bureaucratic models implemented by paid professionals processing their clients impersonally as recipients of social services.

Although five years have passed since the completion of the first draft of this manuscript and six years since the study was completed, my conclusions have not changed but have been fortified by recent events. Despite some talk of "compassion fatigue" enervating Americans, diminishing their empathy with victims, the immediacy and extent of unorganized contributions to Ethiopian famine victims once the first pictures of them were shown on American television in the fall of 1984 showed how empathy is widespread among Americans and can be stirred in crises. The visibility of suffering and the recognition both that the Africans are innocent victims and that one could make an immediate difference to help them through food aid moved many donors. Drives for contributions for food relief became institutionalized in the community through the same organizations that had sponsored and/or helped refugees. Other motives also prompted and reinforced the producers and consumers of national and international rock concerts, the last of which—Band-Aid—drew $20,000,000 for food aid to Africa in 1985, showing how, as I concluded in chapter 5, "Nonaltruistic motives may reinforce altruistic ends and altruistic behavior may be evoked from people who reject altruism once helping becomes the normative thing to do."

Chapter 5 considers how national policy toward types of victims affects attitudes toward helping refugees both in terms of competition for limited resources and the concept of relative deprivation. The more the vision of homeless and hungry Americans is seen, the more congregations are pressed to aid them, especially during a period when governmental assistance is being withdrawn. I propose that the more members of congregations feel relatively deprived because they perceive—correctly or incorrectly—that needy insiders (of their background) are getting less than outsiders, the less they are likely to give others.

A new and more comprehensive survey in 1984 of public attitudes toward immigration and refugee policy illuminated the apparent contradiction between the public opposition to admitting Indochinese refugees and their support for them once they had arrived in 1975 and 1979. Most Americans simply do not distinguish between refugees and immigrants and nine out of ten persons "characterize themselves as either not well informed or having no opinion as to whether refugees should be admitted to the U.S." The more educated and knowledgeable people were, the more likely they were to favor admitting refugees. The majority (52 percent) believed the assertion that "refugees take jobs away from American workers," and 45 percent agreed that "most refugees admitted to the United States wind up on welfare"; they also concurred that these were good reasons not to let in refugees. Yet, when confronted with specific examples of potential refugees and immigrants, majorities agreed that all should be admitted, including examples of political refugees fearing persecution—a Soviet Jew, an Iranian student, a Salvadoran, and a Polish member of Solidarity.

> Especially intriguing about these attitudes toward immigration and refugees, though, is that the public is *less* tolerant at the *more abstract* level, and shows great receptivity as situations become more specific. . . .

Thus, large majorities favored admitting immigrants seeking to be with their children and specific refugees with well-founded fears of persecution. Although two-thirds felt that there were too many foreigners now entering the United States and most cited the belief that refugees take away jobs from American workers, opposition to refugees and immigrants was not related to economic fears, ideological positions, or party identification, but best explained by a "world view hostile to refugees and one that is apparently distrustful of things foreign and that reacts with alarm to the increasing secularization of society."[1]

This makes sense of the popular acceptance of refugees that could not be predicted from the polls (discussed in chapter 2) the greater tendency for the educated public to lead others to welcome them (chapter 3), but does not confirm—or disconfirm—the importance of the sense of relative deprivation (which might be experienced by the poor, the homeless, and minorities) in motivating opposition. Although the survey did not compile responses by income groups, it did show that there was no consistent difference between attitudes of blacks and Hispanics and the general public. It may be that concern over unemployment and job loss is shared among all classes; it may be that such expressed concern often masks an underlying antialien attitude rather than concern for the poor (as was observed by some sponsors themselves in their churches); it may also be that the classes most likely to feel deprived are undersampled in surveys (as are the homeless and telephoneless in this survey) and less likely to vote, correspond with their representatives, and have any visible input in framing public policy. Further research is needed to test how attitudes toward refugees are related to income and ideology.

The question of justice among the needy and evaluation of who is the innocent victim is one we all weigh. Although public empathy and the focus of the conscience constituency may be diverted by government policy, it cannot be dictated to by the federal government. Whether the government's determination that a specific national group of aliens are political refugees and others are not is supported by the public is tested by congregations' willingness to support specific refugees. Although the United States did not admit them as political refugees, over 250 churches and synagogues in 1985 were giving sanctuary to Salvadorans and Guatemalans fleeing lands of widespread political killing, that is, sponsoring them without government permission. Most congregations did not support the Cubans who were finally officially recognized as political refugees in 1980. Many Americans believed that the Cubans were primarily economic refugees, and the Central Americans are primarily political refugees, innocent victims of political persecution and violence. Recent evidence analyzed by William Stanley, which positively relates the fluctuation in the numbers fleeing from El Salvador to the extent of political violence, supports their judgement.[2] The acts of sponsors of Central Americans in the United States in breaking the law (which drew government prosecution in some cases) were justified not just by traditions of religious obligation and nonviolent civil resistance but by their conviction that in giving sanctuary they were implementing the 1980 Refugee Act; they view the U.S. government, by its discriminatory enforcement of the act, as violating the law (see chapter 5). Organizations representing major Protestant and Jewish denominations have endorsed the Sanctuary movement. Yet the cost of helping illegal aliens—one may risk a federal conviction—must deter some helpers. Thus, the politics of recognition of victims in the United States (which so far seems biased against victims of non-Communist regimes) conditions the possibility of mobilizing collective altruism: it is easier to organize followers when authorities concur, but conflicts between the law and conscience means a choice (instead of a fixed deterrent) for the conscience constituency. If we view congregational refugee sponsorship as good for both sponsors and refugees, recognizing the "right to give"—as Titmuss put it—it means that we must reevaluate the rationality and justice of both our domestic and foreign policy.

In recalling now this study was started, I regret I cannot give explicit recognition to the enthusiasts quoted herein, other sponsors, ministers, and the many people who made this movement possible in Riverside County. I especially enjoyed the chance to serve the movement granted me by the Board and members of the Riverside Interfaith Council, and appreciate the active engagement of the Indochinese Refugee Sponsorship Committee and the Director of the RIC, whose cooperation made the task easier. To all of them I owe thanks and appreciation. I am grateful to Charles Glock for his help in classifying religious denominations (in Table 1, chapter 3). I am also grateful to Rusty Kauffman and Hannah Wartenberg for reading earlier versions of this book critically.

I wish to recall the memory of the late Rev. Robert E. Meyer, pastor of the New Paltz Methodist Church and vice-president of New Paltz Citizens Concerned about Indochinese Refugees (CAIR), in dedicating this book. He was a model of caring, compassion, and good sense and humor; besides being a leader, he was never above volunteering for the humblest tasks.

I am also grateful to the editor and Board of Fairleigh Dickinson University Press for the publication of this book.

Congregational Sponsors
of Indochinese Refugees
in the United States, 1979–1981

1

Collective Altruism, Helping, and Lifesaving Behavior

THERE are few instances where people today are given the opportunity to save or directly transform the lives of strangers by their direct actions. The appeal by the major religious denominations of the United States in 1979 to their members to sponsor Indochinese refugees gave congregations a chance to personally renew the lives of those case out without citizenship in any state. They could vote with their hands, heads, hearts, and pocketbooks to affirm that the boat people were people worth saving. They were asked to act in the name of God, of brotherhood, and of neighborliness, but it was an act of altruistic choice: they could be neighbors or bystanders. Their choice (which will later be studied) leads me to explore the meaning and contexts of altruism; why and how do people act for the good of others? Rather than exploring the substantive nature of moral imperatives that prescribe what people ought to do—religious teaching and ethical theory—I am primarily concerned with understanding how and why they act as they do.

Altruism, a term coined by August Comte in 1853 and defined as "regard for others as a principle of action (opposed to egoism or selfishness),"[1] is an elemental and persisting response in social life that has seldom been explored sociologically as emergent behavior before it becomes institutionalized. While definitions of altruism vary, it is easier to agree on what acts are denoted: giving food to the hungry, granting refuge to the outcast, and rescuing or assisting victims of disaster, accident, or assault are usually considered acts of altruism except in cases where one is obligated to do such as a function of role, status, and relationship. The acts of parents in nurturing, feeding, sheltering, and educating their children are not considered acts of altruism but are obligations intrinsic to parenting just as the help rendered by nurse and doctor to the accident victim in the hospital is an obligation of their self-chosen roles.

But behaviors that are now considered altruistic have been a taken-for-granted or normative response in different societies at specific points in time. In early neolithic hunting and gathering societies, sharing the product of the hunt was the rule among all the members of the tribe.[2] The modern socialist ideal of "to each according to his need, from each according to his ability" may not have been the rule in neolithic times if different needs were not recognized, but equality was probably better realized then than it has been since. Such norms of sharing have also been enacted in modern intentional communities—utopias, kibbutzim, communes—whose aim is to generate a new relationship among members based on mutual fulfillment of needs rather than competition.

Altruistic mechanisms may also be built in to traditional societies in order to mitigate inequality. Methods of redistribution and preventing pauperization decreed to be law among the Hebrews in their Torah include the manumission of slaves in the sabbatical (seventh) year, the remission of debts in that year, leaving the fields for gleaners (every year) after the first threshing of grains, and the prohibition of usury among Hebrews. Profit was allowed in loans to foreigners Jewish norms changed, however, during the Hellenistic period (third century Christian Era) when more Jews became engaged in trade, and contemporary Jewish scholars redefined usury to allow Jews to take interest from fellow Jews.[3] Yet the original ideal of Torah still inspired Christian dissidents during the Protestant Reformation who believed they were creating the New Jerusalem.[4]

The question of obligations toward strangers evoked altruistic as well as self-centered concerns in traditional agrarian societies of the Mideast. The issue of granting asylum to the stranger also has biblical antecedents. The history of the Jewish people illustrates the variety of causes moving people to seek asylum outside their community or origin—religious estrangement, famine, political defeat, persecution, political enmity. The Torah instructed the Jews to accord equal treatment to the resident non-Jew or stranger in their midst, although different policies were adopted toward coexistence with tribes and communities with whom they waged wars. The demand for religious conformity as a political rule emerged after Rome adopted Christianity as the state religion and dissidence among Christians was no longer tolerated.[5] The Reformation precipitated persecution because of the principle that the religion of the prince must be the religion of the subject. Modern nation-states have produced the political refugee—victims and enemies of particular regimes. Twentieth-century world wars have magnified their number as massacres and genocide caused whole peoples and collectivities to flee.

Presently, the most universally accepted definition of refugees is that of the United Nations Refugee Convention and Protocol first adopted in 1951: a refugee is one who "owing to well-founded fear of being persecuted for reasons of race, religion, nationality, membership in a particular social group or political opinion" is unable or unwilling to return to his nation of origin or customary residence. This definition has been incorporated in the U.S. Refugee Act of 1980, the first systematic U.S. legislative policy toward refugees. Almost sixteen million people were estimated to be refugees or displaced persons throughout the world in 1980.[6]

The redistribution of income and resources to assist less developed and less wealthy states and the admission of refugees, both one-way transfers, may be the two issues on the international agenda that are most dependent on collective altruism. Many concerned with these issues discuss what ought to be rather than considering what motives might induce donors to make such one-way transfers. Ethical theorists debate the bases for obligation (meaning the obligations of the well-endowed or richer states and classes) in terms of theories of justice;[7] some justify such policies in terms of the enlightened self-interest of the donor. Hardin, however, points to the possibility that sharing will lead to unlimited demand and so deplete our resources that there will be nothing left for sharing.[8] But asserting that there must be limits on collective altruism, weighing the costs and effects, does not deny but implies that collective altruism is a real possibility. Others reject altruism as the basis of social policy, arguing for limits on refugees and immigrants and aid in U.S. national interest, yet take for granted a humanitarian obligation to give emergency relief. Yet, famine and disaster relief, today institutionalized as an international responsibility, was categorically denied as an obligation by Great Britain little more than a century ago during the Irish famine of 1848–49. "Adherence to *laissez-faire* was carried to such a length that in the midst of one of the major famines of history, the government was perpetually nervous of being too good to Ireland and of corrupting the Irish people by kindness and so stifling the virtues of self reliance and industry."[9]

Few social theorists have considered the causes of collective altruism historically or the development of consensus on areas of obligation. Perhaps this is because the dominant ethos of modern individualism focuses attention on the self alone: the model of economic man (and more recently economic woman) looking out for self and family first and weighing the cost of each action rationally in terms of costs and benefits underlies economic theory, political theory, and one trend in social movement theory and has a prominent part in a model of emergency intervention.[10]

Modern society was conceived of by nineteenth-century sociologists (Durkheim, Maine, Toennies, and Weber) as characterized by movements from embeddedness in particular groups based on diffuse but all-encompassing obligations—family, tribe, or community—toward obligations based on specific relationships contracted by the individual engendering new bonds.[11] Sociological theories usually predict that as modernization increases, obligations toward the extended family, tribe, or other collectivity becomes weakened or more variable, as support becomes motivated by sentiment rather than duty. As traditional obligations diminished in the west, exposing the aged, the poor, and the sick who were detached from families to the suffering of makeshift custodial organizations—the poorhouse and the asylum—the newly enfranchised working classes who had borne the burden of the suffering imposed by early capitalism challenged the necessity of their suffering and demanded state responsibility to provide pensions and assistance for the aged, the disabled, the sick, and the unemployed. The endemic class conflicts that Marx anticipated would lead toward revolution were moderated by the evolution of the welfare state, which guaranteed the fulfillment of a collective obligation of all to all.

Yet suspicion of or indifference to the value of altruism may have been an unanticipated consequence of the welfare state and social democracy. The social democratic or paternalistic state made the poor independent of the soup kitchens and hostels of private charity, which were viewed as acts of noblesse oblige or paternalism. Thus altruism, like philanthropy, acquired a bad name by being associated originally with a class order that reiterated the donors' distance and the recipients' dependency. The justification for altruism as voluntary action was diminished by the collective claims of rights of the recipients, of entitlements or equity. If the recipients can demand a good or resource—a pension, hospital care, or food—as a right, the donor of whom it was demanded no longer freely volunteers it, for to volunteer implies the right to withhold it. The issue today is not only entitlements within states among citizens but entitlements between states.

Theories of Altruism

Several questions about altruism arouse reoccurrent argument. Does altruism exist in practice? What type of social action is it? What good does "doing good" do for the doer and for the receiver? What unintended consequences are latent in doing good?

Altruism is seldom studied by sociologists despite the kudos given to Durkheim's classic *Suicide,* focusing on altruistic suicide as a basic type.[12] Besides Durkheim's view of altruism and social integration, both Max Weber's and Talcott Parsons's categories of action recognize that there are other-directed actions for nonutilitarian, affective, idealistic, religious, or "sentimental" ends.[13]

From the viewpoint of the exchange theorists, both the gift and the helping hand are elemental media in social exchange.[14] However, a newer and influential perspective on social action, sociobiology, denies that altruism is other directed.

Altruism, as used by the sociobiologists, is a label for an indirect strategy of "the selfish gene" to perpetuate itself through a genetically linked other.[15] The sociobiologists have confounded the whole question by first reducing altruism to denote acts among kin such as parents giving up their own lives in order to save those of their children, equating these with instances in other species (bees, ants) in which the individual organism is sacrificed to maximize survival of the hive or colony.

Whether this explains (as opposed to labeling) anything but the stereotyped examples from which it is derived so casuistically is open to question. Although the sociobiologists do offer explicit mathematical tests of the short-term biological efficiency of self-sacrifice based on the genetic similarity between the altruist and the beneficiary, they do not usually evaluate whether the behavior of humans traditionally labeled as altruistic can be accounted for by its supposed biologic function. Generally, instances in which people sacrifice themselves for individuals to whom they are not related are ignored, as are instances where people increase the risk for the survival of their own kin by their behavior.

Labeling genetic strategies "egotistic" and "altruistic" is semantic reductionism: ". . . gene behavior is in no sense really selfish or egotistic. . . . The whole appeal of Edward O. Wilson's suggested explanation of ethics seems to stem from metaphors that in the end must be admitted to be question-begging."[16]

Wilson then appeared to redefine altruism and advanced new arguments to deny that it had any benign connotations, while claiming to retain a sociobiological foundation. Wilson distinguished between "soft-core" and "hard-core" altruism, viewing the latter with as much alarm as other critics view pornography (similarly divided by some). Soft-core altruism, according to Wilson, is either reciprocal altruism (self-interested behavior) or hypocritical behavior consciously calculated to enhance the altruist. But hard-core altruism is even worse:

. . . pure, hard-core altruism based on kin selection is the enemy of civilization. If human beings are to a large extent guided by programmed learning rules and canalized emotional development to favor their own relatives and tribe, only a limited amount of global harmony is possible. International cooperation will approach an upper limit, from which it will be knocked down by the perturbations of war and economic struggle, cancelling each upward surge based on pure reason.[17]

Wilson has stretched the concept of kin to group, tribe, and nation: in effect, one's own "kind" has been equated to kin. However, this weakens rather than strengthens sociobiological explanation by admitting that sacrificial behavior is symbolically motivated rather than genetically programmed. According to Wilson, people sacrifice for those who evoke their identification because they share a common language, myth, or collective representations of a common origin or destiny (such as the nation), just as parents sacrifice for a child. But such behavior, like that of parents who nurture and sacrifice for an adopted child as they would for a birth-child, negates the original sociobiological explanation of the genetic origin, function, and persistence of altruism. Both in terms of cultural and adaptive kin, it is not the protoplasm that the donor shares with the beneficiary but their bonds that inspire the giving of self. The sociobiological equation lacks both explanatory and predictive power.

One type of other-directed helpfulness recognized by sociobiologists, economists, and philosophers is reciprocal altruism or mutual aid, a practice institutionalized in many cultures. Turning toward immediate experience, one observes that reciprocal altruism is widely institutionalized in small towns in the United States in volunteer ambulance corps, fire departments, and rescue squads. Nonprofit blood banks that require the recipient (and/or donors in the name of the recipient) to repay blood used in blood or who call on all members for blood contributions regularly are based on reciprocal altruism. Giving a gift in return may also be explained by the universal rule that reappears in free exchanges between strangers (as well as between friends), the norm of reciprocity.[18]

Reciprocal altruism is an effective way of organizing emergency and disaster responses in communities and organizations of limited size today for reasons similar to those that impelled people in hunting bands prior to the neolithic revolution to share risks and meat equally.

"The reason for this [sharing the produce of the hunt] is the same as that which underlies the popularity of insurance in industrial societies: *it is an effective method of spreading risks.*"[19] Similarly, altruistic or other-regarding choices develop spontaneously under certain conditions in an experimental game such as "prisoner's dilemma" in which the subject playing the prisoner under interrogation is given the choice of betraying his accomplice (and the certainty of reward by the police) or may refuse to talk and be convicted by the betrayal of his accomplice or win (if the accomplice also remains silent). These conditions are similar to the actual ones in which reciprocal altruism has most often emerged historically:

altruism must be efficient for both players; the group of players must be small and players must expect similar conditions to develop from time to time over a long period.[20] The need to defend one's home against fire, to obtain blood in an emergency, to get to the hospital speedily in event of an accident are examples of such recurring but unpredictable needs better met by nonprofit organizations based on reciprocal altruism than by the profit-making sector.

Institutions based on reciprocal altruism also emerge when people are isolated and incur needs and risks none can address alone as on a frontier where families cooperate in defense and construction regardless of whether that frontier exists in a community based on capitalistic individualism (such as the nineteenth-century American frontier) or based on egalitarian communism (such as Israeli kibbutzim in the twentieth century). Reciprocal altruism may also be the basis for new institutions and the economic provision of goods and services in industrial societies. Titmuss observed (1971) that reliance on voluntary blood donors who felt rewarded by helping others was a more reliable basis for attracting blood of better quality than was reliance on profit-making blood banks or on a mixed system.[21]

The Rationality and Limits of Altruism

Are such institutions simply a rational device for economic exchange? If so, it would be "rational" for each individual to delay giving or measure his gift against his reward. Yet some give to such organizations out of proportion to any reward and often such organizations develop their own esprit d'corps, evoking other motives for giving. Collard observes that these are rather simple cases of social exchange rather than economic exchange, citing Peter Blau's criteria: social exchanges "involve the principle that one person does another a favour, and while there is some general expectation of some future return, its exact nature is definitely *not* stipulated in advance."[22] The norm of reciprocity that underlies interaction both exerts authority in its own right and motivates both parties to live up to expectations to keep the relationship going. In Gouldner's archetypical exchange between strangers, were the recipient never to give another gift to the giver, the giver would be disappointed as much because the recipient's violation of the rule meant the relationship couldn't continue as because he had not been rewarded in kind.[23] It seems plausible to conclude that institutions based on reciprocal altruism motivate other-directed behavior among donors, although some may be moved solely by egotism, considering giving a wise investment, and others by fear of social sanction for not giving.

A recurring fallacy that prevents consideration of the real potential (and limits) of altruism is the contention that altruism does not exist at all because all behavior is self-interested basically. The historic controversies about this turn on a false opposition between the objectives of action— "for what end is it intended?"—and the motives or rewards of action ("what does the donor do it for?"). One does not necessarily diminish the good to another by deriving pleasure, satisfaction, and recognition from doing good.

Theoretically, the same range of explanations that is used to explain organized social behavior could explain other-directed behavior or "doing good": one could be coerced or constrained to do good, one could be moved by self-interest or expectations of a return in exchange, or one could be moved by one's own values, being satisfied by feeling good because one had acted in accord with the dictates of transcendant authority, one's conscience, or one's need.

One is confronted by the fact that human beings have accepted widely divergent orders and legitimations of obligation toward others at different epochs in history and different points in the same epoch: they may constrict their obligations to self and kin and engage in social interaction primarily to get the most gain for themselves in exchange; they may voluntarily give time, money, and resources to help others; or they may feel obliged to share equally with others or to give back to them or diminish their advantage for the gain of another. They may turn away from the refugee and the victim; they may give their lives for another.

Yet, despite the wide variety of evidence, the predominant contemporary attitude is skeptical. Skepticism about the potential for altruism and the basis for human cooperation is not new but has been repeatedly justified in the last 200 years by pseudoscientific theories. Darwin's observation that competition *between* species was a fact of nature was distorted by Herbert Spencer and other nineteenth-century "social Darwinists" to justify competition among humans (within species) as a natural law.[24] This was used to produce theories of racial inequality that justified national, colonial, and racial domination. Modern sociobiological explanations for ethnocentrism and group discrimination update the earlier biosociological conventional wisdom (based on dubious and flawed findings), which explained competition and inequality as a product of the natural order.[25]

By contrast with the nineteenth-century schools that provided intellectual legitimation for restricting human sympathy to one's own kind, class, or race, other nineteenth-century social philosophers related theories of human progress to expectations of an expanding universe of obligation. Comte prophecied that the object of feeling would expand outward from the family to the (human) race as a result of social evolution. "Or, as he puts it in other words, altruism in antiquity is domestic and civic, the the Middle ages it is collective, and in the positive period (forthcoming) it is universal."[26] Kropotkin, an influential moral philosopher, asserted that helpfulness was not based on altruism or love but here was a "law of mutual aid" that developed with the evolution of our species because it enhanced chances of survival, a law apprehended intuitively.[27]

The historical record of the nineteenth and twentieth centuries does not reveal any clear pattern of unilineal development to support such a thesis. Both nineteenth-century democratic nationalism and Marxist internationalism assumed national and class liberation would lead toward greater empathy and cooperation between peoples rather than conflict. Paradoxes between national and class behavior and intellectual thought and social movements abound. Shortly after the triumph of the antislavery movement, imperialism and ideologies of race justifying white supremacy expanded western influence throughout the world. The massive violence of the twentieth century reached its zenith with the genocide of the Holocaust produced by Nazi Germany: the Holocaust and the mass murders resulting from state socialism have been followed by covenants of universal human rights, more genocides, and the diffusion of torture around the globe.

For many, the collective violence of the twentieth century has obscured any vision of altruism except as deviant or exceptional behavior. The capacity or will of people to respond to neighbors (and strangers) in trouble in everyday life has also become problematic as urban dwellers become more vulnerable to becoming victims of crime because they do not come to each other's aid (exemplified by the rape-murder in New York City in 1964 of Kitty Genovese whose cries for help were overheard by 38 neighbors who failed to act).

One many raise the first question of why people help others on an individual level: what is known about how, when, and why individuals voluntarily aid those in need or trouble? Evidence is drawn from studies of people who help others voluntarily and from laboratory and naturalistic experiments devised by social psychologists to test whether people will help another person. (After this, I shall inquire about how to study altruism as collective or organized behavior.)

Studying Altruism and Helping Behavior: The Interdependence of Definition, Theory, and Findings

There has been much social psychological research to determine why and when people assist others in trouble that was reviewed by Staub.[28] Differences in response can first be attributed to whether people perceive and recognize that the sufferer is an innocent victim. People may maintain their belief that this is a just world in which one gets what one deserves by attributing responsibility or assigning blame to the victim. Second, the likelihood of an individual helping is related to whether an appeal or signal for help is clearly addressed to one person or whether the responsibility for helping is diffused, as is a signal apprehended by a crowd; the latter is less likely to unite people to act. Third, risks and rewards are weighed: these include the costs of aiding the victim, the observability of helping or failing to help, and the rewards for helping, such as social recognition and approval, which may be expected.

Empathy and prosocial values also have been related to readiness to aid victims. But empathy is itself related to beliefs, values, and orientations toward the other, which predispose people toward identification. Staub observes:

> Most people learn some degree of identification with others who are members of the same "in-group." One influence on prosocial behavior must be how narrowly or broadly an in-group is defined. A child may learn either that only his or her family or that also his or her tribe or religious or racial group or people of the same nationality are also like him or are reasonable objects for identification.[29]

One question of great contemporary concern is whether and why a bystander will help a person in need: a neighbor, a passer-by, or a stranger. There are many alternative theoretical explanations of empathy and helping behavior based on sociobiology, theories about learning, cognitive-development, and equity and psychoanalysis.[30] Piliavin and her coauthors review studies of emergency intervention in order to test a model explaining why people help others in chance situations—accidents, disasters, health emergencies, criminal assaults and so on.[31] They posit and show that the evidence is consistent with a model of an onlooker aroused by a new event that must be simultaneously defined and evaluated, weighing the costs and rewards for direct intervention (and the alternatives) before responding. Yet, there is evidence that the whole process may be shortcircuited by the onlooker who becomes extremely aroused in a situation demanding an immediate response for help to be effective. The onlooker may respond impulsively without weighing costs, regardless of his or her closeness or similarity to the victim. Where onlookers are members of a crowd, and responsibility to intervene is diffused, they are less likely to intervene impulsively than when they are confronted by the victim alone.

Thus, it is the discomfort of the onlooker or bystander that is the first cause in their model although all variables interact or impact upon each other. The authors define altruistic behavior idiosyncratically as "behavior *motivated solely by the desire to benefit another without the possibility of rewards for the self*" [my italics], while admitting the difficulty with this definition: "Since some internalized system of self-reward is always a possibility, any behavior, no matter now objectively costly to the self and beneficial to another, and no matter now deliberately decided upon, can be interpreted as selfish. . . ."[32]

Although Piliavin et al. review research showing how helping behavior is related to the acceptance or denial by the onlooker of norms of social responsibility entailing personal obligation, they tend to reduce the impact of values and norms to "the cost-benefit framework [which is] quite consistent with the model."[33] Emotional involvement in fulfilling such norms is reduced to the cost of discomfort versus the reward of heightened self-esteem: "That is, people help because they will feel bad about themselves if they do not act and will feel good about themselves if they do."[34] Since no act exemplifies their definition as all action evokes good or bad feelings, altruism is denied by semantic fiat. Nevertheless they conclude that "we-ness"—identification with the victim (usually evoked by likeness)—can both influence perceived costs and rewards and intensify arousal to the point that costs are not even considered.[35]

The paradox implied in the conventional definition of altruism was observed by Lester Ward in 1883:

> The egoistic basis of altruism is the great moral paradox. All actions emanate from feelings of some kind, and these must all agree in having pleasure for their end. In their ultimate analysis, therefore, all actions spring from the same motive. The real distinction between egoism and altruism must be looked for at a later stage in the development of motives. . . . It is certainly a fact that the recognition of suffering in others is attended, to different degrees in different individuals, and in very close proportion to the grade of physical and mental organization, with a corresponding painful sensation. It is upon this unquestionable truth that the egoistic quality of so-called altruistic action rests.[36]

Merton reiterates the view of Charles H. Cooley that "All social sentiments are altruistic in the sense that they involve reference to another person; few are so in the sense that they exclude the self." Merton concludes "that when Comte coined the term 'altruism' and defined it as he did, he helped create the kind of fallacy which Cooley tried to counteract."[37]

Many researchers avoid the definitional issue by the study of "prosocial," "cooperative," or "helping" behavior. Macauley and Berkowitz reviewed the range of answers to:

> What is "altruism"? For Darley and Latane, the researchable question really is "What determines, in a particular situation, whether or not one person helps another in distress?" By implication in this definition, any behavior which benefits another in need, regardless of the helper's motives, is altruistic. A very different kind of answer to this question is given by Aronfreed. He identifies a basic motive for altruism and confines usage of the term to behavior which meets this motivational standard.[38]

Aronfreed's definition is worth bearing in mind through this research, for it resolves the altruistic paradox by assuming that expected benefit to the other is independent of but does not exclude self-reward.

> The concept of altruism can more usefully be restricted to the choice of an act which is at least partly determined by the actor's expectation of consequences which will benefit another person without benefit to himself. But the expected consequences for the other person are not necessarily without affective (and reinforcement) value for the actor, even though directly beneficial outcomes for the actor are not specified by the altruistic component of the act . . . changes of self-esteem or other consequences of self-evaluation cannot have a criterial status in the specification of the affective or cognitive mechanisms of altruistic behavior.[39]

Studies of Helping People: From "Good Neighbors" to Lifesavers

Besides studies of individuals and incidents (natural or constructed in laboratories), there are a few studies of people who actually volunteer to help others who are troubled, disabled, discriminated against, or persecuted. These people differ from people who are usually helpful by going out of their way to help strangers, including strangers belonging to stigmatized or oppressed minorities. One may ask: what are the characteristics of these people and what motivates them?

Pitirim A. Sorokin pioneered in sociological research on altruists as individuals in *Altruistic Love*.[40] The good neighbors were recommended in letters to a radio program soliciting such stories: they were people who succored the lonely, helped the handicapped, and visited the homebound, using much of their leisure time to respond to people in need in warm, nonroutinized ways without being asked. He viewed them as deviates because of their hyperconformity to the Golden Rule. "Asked to state what factors they ascribed their good neighborliness, 21 percent indicated religion; 29 percent, parental and family training; 8 percent, school education; 3 percent, unusual specific experience . . .; 28 percent, universal life experience (the cooperative character of human nature). . . ."[41] Otherwise, they were undistinguished or distinguished only by their personal integration. There were likely to come from the middle class, have had a happy childhood, report their parental homes were well integrated and more likely to be married and have slightly larger families (reported to be harmonious and well integrated) than other Americans at that time. They were not only engaged in individual good works, but were fully involved in community activities. Sorokin relates that "every 'good neighbor' is a member of several—at least five—organizations."[42] The majority, who were women, belong to service groups, social organizations, and women's clubs.

Sorokin's "good neighbors" usually elicited only positive recognition from their neighbors, but there are helpers who enabled others to attain their rights who received and might expect punishment from their neighbors such as the Freedom Riders who helped integrate buses in the southern United States during the early 1960s. David Rosenham compared fully and partially committed activists—both blacks and whites—who had been involved in demonstrations organized by the civil rights movement in the northeast up to 1961 (prefacing the period of continuing confrontations, front-page publicity, and widespread involvement in the movement).[43] What can one say about people who do good who may not be rewarded or may be punished? Rosenham's activists were not dissimilar to Sorokin's "good neighbors"; the fully committed were more influenced by a parent as a moral model—coming from homes in which there was warmth and tolerance, with parents who taught them to act on their beliefs by personal example—and were less conflicted and mentally healthier people than the partially committed.

Rosenham makes a useful distinction between "autonomous altruism," such as the acts of these activists, and "normative altruism"—habitual or institutionalized responses to people in need—"giving a few dollars to the Heart Fund, offering a lady a seat on the bus, giving a stranger directions or a hitch, helping someone with a flat tire, and returning a lost wallet," which are usually low-cost and low-risk acts.[44] Sorokin's "good neighbors" were predominantly autonomous altruists who risked little and elicited much social approval. Rosenham's Freedom Riders were autonomous altruists who often risked physical battery, evoking widespread approval from the partially committed and virulent hatred from the supporters of white supremacy.

Even greater risks were taken by the twenty-seven "rescuers" of Jews in hiding during the Holocaust studied by Perry London.[45] These were individuals operating on their own in countries in which social defense networks to help Jews did not exist or emerged too late to help most. In many instances such people scarcely knew of other helpers and feared that friends and neighbors might betray them to the police and occupation authorities in states where German authority was buttressed by native collaboration. London's fragmentary study (he regards it as incomplete) showed that the rescuers had little in common. Some undertook risks knowledgeably; some just fell into it without forethought. Some were paid for services and others spent fortunes, leaving themselves destitute. "Some rescuers were fanatically religious, others were devout atheists. Some were deeply affiliated with Jews, others were anti-Semitic. An on and on."[46] The only common characteristics found were "a zest for adventure," strong identification with a parent as a moral model, and an experience of social marginality—for example, membership in a political or religious minority. "Some kind of active moralism seemed characteristic of all the rescuers and usually was related to parental morality rather than to a specific kind of ideology."[47]

A report by Fogelman and Weiner of research on helpers of Jews identified their two most prevalent characteristics as "risk-tolerance" (ability to transcend fear) and identification with a parent who had been altruistic.[48] A study by Grossman based on nine—most of whom were publicly recognized—helpers showed that the commonality in childhood was based on the absence of violence on the part of parents and their expression of affection and communication. This led to their children's self-acceptance and to their later ability to take risks and become their own authority when they realized Jews might be murdered if they did not act. Grossman compared this to postwar studies of German anti-Nazis (comparing their childhood to the assumed typical German authoritarian pattern) and found the findings consistent with hers.[49]

The most comprehensive survey of people who helped Jews survive during the Holocaust is Nechama Tec's study of Polish rescuers. Tec concludes that the essential distinguishing characteristic of all is that they were autonomous altruists: individualists (or marginal in London's terms), accustomed "to act in accordance with personal convictions, . . . [with a] broad and long-lasting commitment to stand up for the helpless and needy . . . [who shared] universalistic perceptions of Jews that defined them [at the time] as helpless beings and as totally dependent on the protection of others."[50] She notes, too, how they denied and minimized the risk.

Tec's study is more analytical and systematic than earlier studies and the many journalistic accounts of individual rescuers, many of whom have been recognized as "righteous gentiles" by Yad Vashem, the Israeli Holocaust memorial authority. All of these studies suggest that one underlying attribute of the rescuers is that they believed they were responsible for others, viewed Jews as victims, and internalized a universalistic framework of moral obligation.

Despite the intrinsic interest and significance of these studies, they may be misleading if one is concerned with why people collectively help others. For they imply that all helpers were autonomous altruists taking the same degree of risk (high) and overlook the varying political contexts and the degree of social approval and organization of helping behavior, assuming it was always perilous, isolated, and deviant activity. Singular individuals engaged in research did little to undermine the machinery of destruction as long as they were an isolated atomized minority without social organization.

And leaders such as Father Benoit (interviewed by Grossman), who mobilized a social defense movement to help Jews avoid victimization in France and Italy, did not act alone.[51] While the leaders of such social defense movements appear to be autonomous altruists—innovators and risk-takers who define the situation for themselves—the more the movement spreads, the more it is likely to attract normative altruists. This in turn, reduces the risk of helping, for the spread of the movement means there are fewer potential collaborators who might betray the helper, and they are more likely to desist if they fear the movement's censure or sanction.

Social defense movements may represent whole subcultures or communities. Even in the Holocaust there were communities and nations who sided with the victims, enabling the majority to evade being caught in the Nazi net.[52] This enables one to learn how altruistic or helping behavior emerges from social organization and structure. In the next chapter, I shall explore the development and organization of collective defenses that enabled the Jews to avoid becoming victims in certain places, the emergent character of the pregenocidal phases of victimization, and the critical significance of refugee crises as a testing process. I shall also discuss how response to the Indochinese refugee crisis of 1978–79 was related to the response to the forced exodus of German Jewry in 1938–39.

2

Collective Altruism, Refugee and Rescue Policy:
The Holocaust and the 1979 Crisis

THE refugee who is cast out of a state because of politics, membership in an unwanted religious, national, racial, or ethnic group, or social class may be the prototypical figure of the victim of the twentieth century. In the wake of the Allied victory in World War II, almost 250,000 Jews who were liberated from German extermination and concentration camps or had escaped the Nazi net fled states in which they found they could not go home again; about a million East European people fled the newly Soviet-dominated satellites; more than 12.4 million people of German extraction were expelled from Poland, Czechoslovakia, Hungary, and Yugoslavia.[1] Anticolonial struggles and conflicts over the transfer of power in divided societies led to the exodus of about 1.4 million French and almost all Jewish Algerians in 1962 and 10.5 million minority-group members in the Indian subcontinent in 1947, Hindus fleeing for their lives from Pakistan and Muslims streaming there for safety as genocidal assaults claimed perhaps half a million victims.[2] Nationalistic regimes may expel "outsiders"—an ethnic group of foreign origin—in order to redistribute the spoils, as Idi Amin expelled the Indians from Uganda in 1972. "Middleman minorities" who traditionally engage in trade—overseas Chinese, Greeks, Indians, Jews—or "alien pariahs" are particularly vulnerable to such persecution.[3]

32

Some of these peoples were viewed by outsiders as innocent victims, while others were seen as receiving their just desserts for the role they had played. Both were ejected by similar measures: massacres, state threats and discrimination, and the realistic apprehension of greater losses in the future usually provoke refugees to flee. The state provoking their flight may be satisfied with getting rid of some or may continue to oppress the others remaining, either to drive them to leave or to assimilate them by making it impossible to perpetuate their distinctive ethnic identity. Another, and fatal, possibility was illustrated by Nazi Germany in which the state's goal of eliminating the Jews by forced emigration was transformed to the "Final Solution of the Jewish Question" by annihilation.

While the refugees' most immediate problem may be to escape violence and find physical security if they cannot return—and some may look to coups and civil wars to enable them to come home—their long-range problem begins with their juridical status. If a class of people are deprived of citizenship and thus excluded by the nation-state, they are in a social void in a world of nation-states unless recertified by other nation-states (although they may now be temporarily protected by the UN High Commissioner of Refugees and the United Nations Relief and Rehabilitation Administration [UNRRA]). Some refugees already have an alternate status as citizens of another state or claims against a state that must certify them as citizens; these have included the Indians in Uganda who held British passports, the *pieds noirs* of Algeria who were French citizens, and Jews expelled from Iraq and Algeria after 1948 who were entitled to Israeli citizenship. Other refugees may be able to infiltrate a neighboring state; however, their ultimate security depends on legalization of their entry. Thus the refugee who constitutes the "other"—the noncitizen, the stranger—tests the nation-state's commitment to helping those toward whom they have no obligation. If the state has a traditional closed door or selective policy toward immigrants (based on national or ethnic quotas, immigrants' skills, national needs, and so on), the state has the choice of either opening the door or keeping it shut (or half-shut); if the state has a traditional open door, it may leave it open or close it.

However, the decision to take in refugees is just the first step. Refugees imply costs: they must be fed, housed, clothed, taught how to adapt themselves and assimilate into the economy if they are not to be a permanent dependent population. In the long run, refugees may become an economic asset rather than a deficit, but political leaders and citizens are apt to see outlays for refugees as a one-way flow of money. If seen in this way, taking in refugees is fundamentally an act of collective altruism.

Yet not taking in refugees also may imply or provoke costs for which state leaders may wish to avoid responsibility. If refugees are fleeing a genocidal assault, failure to help them means that one is also responsible for their deaths and the deaths of others who may come after them. Further, failure to harbor refugees is a violation of international law: the UN Convention of 1951 and Protocol of 1967 prohibit the expulsion of return of a refugee "to the frontiers of territories where his life or freedom would be threatened on account of his race, religion, nationality, membership in a particular social group or political opinion."[4] Failure to protest genocidal assaults and invasions of human rights may be seen by the violator as a sign of tolerance and signal that nothing will be done to stop them, and may escalate the likelihood of genocide and massacre. Both domestic constituencies and other countries may castigate the political leadership that overlooks this and turns aside from the victims.

Apart from the state, voluntary organizations committed to foreign and humanitarian service and other organizations and movements (churches, labor, parties) have interests and values at issue. The impact of mass public opinion may be a factor taken into account by leaders. There also are special constituencies more likely to mobilize on behalf of particular groups of refugees based on ethnic identification. One may also now look toward a "conscience constituency" or leadership elite (more likely to be drawn from the educated classes in western nations) who are concerned about human rights issues as potential actors.[5] Thus, leaders' decisions can be related to the expected costs of enacting the policies desired by particular constituencies and elites as well as the costs of taking in refugees. Besides these, leaders' conception of "national interest," their anticipation of the opinions of foreign governments and elites, and their apprehensions of the costs and impact of just standing by and refusing to help are factors bearing on their decisions.

Looking backward, one does not observe the cause of states' action or inaction during refugee crises as much as the consequences. Focusing first on the Holocaust and pre-Holocaust refugee emergency can enable one to observe how the roles of the bystander changed along with the options and destiny of the victims and observe the levels at which helping or lifesaving behavior was possible. In no way does this claim to be a summary history of that period or to cite all possibilities and attempts previously documented;[6] rather, I focus on a selected number of relevant cases and experiences.

Helping before and during the Holocaust

The critical actors in the Holocaust are usually depicted as victimizers, victims, and bystanders. The bystanders have been identified as the other nation-states occupied by or allied to Nazi Germany; in fact, some states were victimizers, some victims; there were willing and resistant bystanders. The pivotal actors within the state were those organizations and movements which might mobilize solidarity with the Jews—the churches and resistance movements—other free associations, and the state bureaucracy itself. In some states Jews themselves—as individuals, as a collectivity, and in organizations—played a significant role in evoking or organizing resistance.

Before World War II, Germany's goal was to force the emigration of German and Austrian Jewry, after stripping them of their rights, offices, and real and personal property. After 1939, Jews in German-occupied Europe and Axis satellites were progressively detached—defined as a special class of noncitizens, stripped of rights, statuses, and goods— segregated (socially labeled with the yellow star), and isolated by concentration in ghetto and camp. Thus, they were readily seized, gassed, and incinerated after the implementation of "the Final Solution" in 1941. Where Jews had previously been excluded and were morally isolated by fellow natives, they might be segregated, seized, and massacred in days; in western Europe, the process took years.

Three types of opportunity were presented to the bystanders at different points in time for saving the Jews (besides deterring the aggression of Nazi Germany and its violation of the rights of its Jewish citizens before 1939 by diplomatic and political prewar strategies other than those used). First, more Jews would have escaped annihilation had states enabled them to emigrate outside of continental Europe between 1933 and 1941. The Allies also could have assisted and encouraged legal and illegal exodus of Jews from Axis-occupied and allied Europe from 1941 to 1945. Second, their right to be could have been defended within the nations where they were between 1941 and 1945 by social defense movements that arose to deter deportations or help Jews evade being caught. Third, the annihilation of some Jews might have been blocked during World War II by the Allies' physical attack on the machinery of destruction—the extermination camps and rail lines leading to them—and the Allies' use of the full range of sanctions and incentives to deter deportations by German-allied states. These three strategies—refugee aid and rescue, deterrence of and social defense against deportations, and direct (and indirect) action to disable the machinery of destruction—were never fully exploited.

How does one account for how little was done? To answer this indirectly, I will scan the underlying sources of inaction in democratic nations, focusing on the United States, and examine the characteristics of nations or communities that helped Jews. Although Germany's denial of citizenship to German Jews in 1935 (the Nuremberg laws) and physical violence against Jews (culminating in the state-instigated Krystallnacht "pogrom" in 1938) was well publicized in the west, it did not provoke affirmative counteractions. As Hannah Arendt put it:

The calamity of the rightless is . . . not that they are not equal before the law, but no law exists for them. . . . Only in the last stage of a rather lengthy process is their right to live threatened. . . . Even the Nazis started their extermination of Jews by first depriving them of all legal status . . . and cutting them off from the world of the living by herding them into ghettoes and concentration camps; and before they set the gas chambers into motion they had carefully tested the ground and found out to their satisfaction that no country would claim these people.[7]

The first prerequisite for taking in Jewish refugees (presuming one must open a closed door) was acknowledging that the Jews were victims who were unjustly persecuted. The second was acceptance by other states of responsibility for redressing their plight and willingness to pay the expected costs (real or imaginary) of increased immigration. Neither was present. My thesis is that the effect of propaganda about the "Jewish problem" over decades was to convince people that the Jews were the cause of the problem; ergo, they could not be viewed as innocent victims. Germany's solution of the "Jewish questions" was regarded by both the United States and Great Britain as an internal affair before World War II— a matter of concern only insofar was Germany generated Jewish refugees leading to pressure for sanctuary.

President Roosevelt refused to recognize that Jews were special victims of German persecution before the war, preferring to recognize only "political refugees," and in 1938 privately proposed a quota on Jewish refugees.[8] Similarly, he proposed in 1943 at the Casablanca conference, which considered Allied policies in liberated North Africa, that Jews be limited in the professions by quotas: "The President stated that his plans would further eliminate the specific and understandable complaints which the Germans bore toward the Jews in Germany."[9] Not until 1944 did President Roosevelt publicly recognize that Jews were special victims of German policy.

Governing elites in the U.S. State Department and the British Foreign Office were either anti-Semitic and/or anxious to disavow Nazi allegations about Jewish influence and to deny any positive identification with the Jews.[10] Officials often blamed the Jews for their plight, as did almost three out of five Americans polled in 1938, who held the European Jews responsible in some measure for their persecution.[11]

The western world had been given a prolonged opportunity to help the Jews evade victimization before the Holocaust when Germany's policy was to expel, not exterminate, German Jews; nation after nation refused to alter their immigration policy to take in Jewish refugees, culminating in the Evian conference on refugees in 1938, which "interested and disinterested spectators alike saw . . . as an exercise in Anglo-American collaborative hypocrisy." One German newspaper observed that "the conference serves to justify Germany's policy against Jewry."[12] The uniform restrictive immigration policies of this period have been attributed to fear of economic competition and xenophobia as well as anti-Semitism. Some nations at Evian also justified their opposition to taking in Jewish refugees by their desire to avoid creating a "Jewish problem."[13] In other states there were similar restrictions. No state allowed entry of more than four Jewish refugees per thousand state population between 1933 and 1945 except Palestine, which took in 105.4 per thousand and would have accepted more had not the mandating power, Great Britain, limited Jewish immigration. In the safer havens of rescue in the Americas, the ratio of Jewish refugees accepted between 1933 and 1945 ranged from 0.8 per thousand (Canada) to 2.1 per thousand (Argentina).[14]

Looking at the United States as the most desired and safest haven outside Europe, one may ask, where was the constituency one might expect to identify with the victims? The lack of mobilization by American Jewish leaders in a united drive to save the Jews of Europe demands explanation. One can attribute this both to organizational conflicts and to ideologies among them that denied the legitimacy of Jewish self-interest, thus preventing mainstream Jewish organizations from demanding that the United States take in German Jews; these ideologies reflected the defensive response of American Jews to their perception of anti-Semitism in the United States, leading Jews to try to rebut the accusations of their enemies by denial rather than the assertion of specific Jewish interests and demands.[15] The chairman of the American Jewish Commission on the Holocaust, Arthur Goldberg, and Rabbi Arthur Hertzberg, drew similar conclusions as they reflected on the causes of the failure of American Jewry:

> . . . world Jewry and especially, the American Jews, the only major community relatively untouched by the war, should have raised an outcry, day after day, that would have pierced the prevailing indifference. . . . That it did not do so, was not, however, caused by the immediate, all too usual failures of organization. . . .This failure belonged not alone to the organizations' leaders but to American Jewry as a whole. . . . American Jewry was thus in a *double trap*, made up of its fears for itself, in a still anti-semitic America, and of its cautious political attitudes, fashioned by many centuries of Diaspora.[16]

David Wyman has also shown that the struggle between Jewish factions geared toward different postwar visions—Zionist and non-Zionist—negated the possibility for uniting and mobilizing all the energy, numbers, and resources of American Jews on behalf of the immediate rescue of European Jewry and deterring further extermination.[17]

Before knowledge of the Final Solution was acknowledged (December 1942) by the Allies, there was little concern and support for Jewish refugees among potential allies. American church leaders who protested anti-Jewish discrimination and gave public support were likely to be on the national level and were unable to mobilize support or resources at the grass-roots level. Christian allies also counseled caution in pressing Jewish claims, which diminished Jewish leadership's confidence in the possibility of achieving anything.[18] To be sure, there was a general lack of sympathy and unwillingness to bear costs of any refugees on the part of the prewar American public. In fact, Christian leaders in the United States could hardly gather any money for Christian refugees in 1934.[19]

Yet, despite prior overwhelming opposition toward taking in refugees, in 1940 one U.S. poll showed there was a predominantly positive attitude toward taking in British and French "refugee women and children."[20] One does not know whether this can be ascribed to the fact that the German threat was more evident in 1940, that there was a positive predisposition toward these two nations, or that women and children are deemed inherently to be innocent victims while political refugees are not conceived of as innocent.

Prominent Protestant leaders did protest Nazi persecution of Jews from 1939 onward and related this to the Protestant church struggle against the Nazi-inspired "German Christians," but their major concern was with the latter, and Protestant periodicals seldom noted how the United States denied a haven to Jewish refugees.[21] Wyman concludes, that:

> One reason for the government's limited action was the indifference of much of the non-Jewish public. It must be recognized, though, that many Christian Americans were deeply concerned about the murder of European Jewry . . . [but] America's Christian churches were almost inert in the face of the Holocaust and nearly silent too. No major denomination spoke out on the issue. Few of the many Christian publications cried out for aid to the Jews. Few even reported the news of the extermination, except infrequently and incidentally.[22]

Thus, there was no national constituency mobilized to save the European Jews that could counter the official bureaucracy and the well-organized opponents of immigration at the time when it could have counted the most. Even after the Allies officially recognized the German annihilation of the European Jews and promised postwar response (December 1942), there was insufficient pressure to compel the official bureaucracy to use national resources in the United States and Great Britain to check "the Final Solution."

A national organization of prominent public figures, the Emergency Committee to Save the Jewish People, emerged in the United States in 1943, instigated by a small cadre of Palestinian Jews, former emissaries of the Irgun, who were rejected and attacked by U. S. mainstream Zionist leaders who wanted to maintain control over the direction and leadership of U. S. Jewry.[23] The Emergency Committee was among the forces that successfully pressed President Roosevelt to establish the War Refugee Board (WRB) in 1944 to deter "Nazi plans to exterminate all the Jews." Nevertheless, despite this avowed goal, the United States refused to take direct action to bomb the extermination camps and rail lines leading to them despite their demonstrated capacity to do so in 1944, pleading (falsely) technical inability.[24] Similarly, in Great Britain, the bureaucracy detoured implementation of a request by the War Cabinet to make plans to bomb the camps, and the Soviet Union rejected a WRB request to liberate Auschwitz.[25] Thus, all major Allies rejected using the force at their command for direct action to abort further annihilation of the European Jews in 1944; saving the Jews was not their objective; it did not justify to them the use of intelligence, material, and manpower.

During the Holocaust the question in Europe was the defense of the Jews of one's own nation. Identification with the victim depended not only on acknowledgment that they were victims but on including them *earlier* in a common "universe of obligation—that circle of persons toward whom obligations are owed, to whom the rules apply, and whose injury calls for expiation by the community."[26] *Accounting for Genocide*, a study of national differences in the magnitude of Jewish victimization during the Holocaust, proposed (among other hypotheses) that the earlier exclusion of the Jews from a common universe of obligation (demonstrated by the prewar success of anti-Semitic movements) would be positively related to the percent of Jews caught in each state. This was largely confirmed. "The more successful were pre-war anti-Semitic movements, the more Jewish victims there were."[27]

But social defense of the Jews was not a consequence of a negative fact—the lack of institutionalized anti-Semitism—or even of anti–anti-Semitism alone but of positive social organization. Effective defense never emerged spontaneously as an expression of popular attitudes or mass independent actions but was a product of mobilization by social authorities who defined the situation so as to justify subversion of German edicts or the laws of their own state and organized lifesaving networks enabling the potential victims to live in hiding, counterfeit a non-Jewish identity, or escape. Church leaders were often principal instigators. Although there were prominent leaders of dominant churches who failed to publicly protest (such as Pope Pius XII) and others who collaborated with or overlooked the destruction of the Jews, there were also church leaders in other countries who publicly acknowledged that the Jews were their brothers as well as innocent victims. Their sermons and example justified obedience to a higher law and disobedience to secular edicts.

How such defense movements emerged can be illustrated by examining Denmark, a state in which the whole community constituting the nation organized itself against the German action, and Le Chambon sur Lignon (France), a community in opposition to French and German authorities' seizure of the Jews. What one can learn from Denmark—a well-known case of resistance—has been obscured by widespread myths attributing the saving of Danish Jewry to the king who wore the yellow star. No yellow-star order was introduced in Denmark, and the king has been bestowed the plaudits belonging to the whole nation. To understand what happened, one must also understand the political status of Denmark during World War II.

Denmark was a self-governing neutral acceding to German demands for military cooperation from April 1940 to November 1942, when German authority was reinforced. Yet free parliamentary elections were held in March 1943, in which the pro-Nazi party got only 3 percent of the vote. No anti-Semitic legislation discriminating, segregating, and labeling the Jews with the yellow star had been tolerated in self-governing Denmark, as had been imposed in occupied Europe, so the 7,700 Danish and foreign Jews in Denmark were less vulnerable to apprehension than were Jews in other German-occupied states. A German ultimatum to repress resistance activity provoked the Danish government to resign in August 1943. The Germans then assumed military command and declared a state of emergency.

The German decision to catch the Jews of Denmark was precipitated by rivalry between German forces, a leader of which indirectly informed prominent Danes of the planned raid; the latter tipped off Jewish community leaders. But the Danes' decision to defend the Jews was based on an earlier resolve on which there was a consensus of all Danish authorities, including the Danish Lutheran church, which had protested anti-Semitism even before the war. Yahil observes:

> On this point there was no divergence between the attitudes of Danish officialdom and of the underground movement. There was not the slightest disagreement with the view that the rights and lives of the Jews had to be protected. . . . what is significant here is that for the Danes *national consciousness and democratic consciousness are one and the same.* . . . and all citizens constitute a mutual guarantee to one another that these principals will be maintained. . . . The struggle of the Danish people for its national existence during the occupation therefore included the struggle for the equal rights of the Jews.[28]

News of the raid on the night of 1–2 October 1943—broadcast from pulpits through Denmark the next Sunday—instigated protests from virtually all Danish churches, parties, and associations. The Freedom Council, the coordinating resistance organization, decided that the Jews had to leave Denmark to evade the Nazi net for the duration of the war and organized the flight to Sweden over a sea route that had not previously been used for escape and was patrolled by the German navy. Networks of helpers were organized by locality in the seaside villages that were departure points and by profession (teachers, doctors, priests, journalists, and student rings) in Copenhagen. These rings discovered, hid, supported, and transported the Jews during their exodus and arranged payment to the fishermen who risked losing their craft if caught. The movement was not an underground movement whose members must conceal their activities from their own neighbors, for cooperation was so unified that organizations could openly plan how to exploit their resources for the task at hand: the hospitals used their ambulances to convey Jews to the coast and staffs met daily to plan schedules.

> Unlike most social movements in opposition, it was tolerated or supported by Danish officials (at different levels). Danish ministers broadcast warnings to their parishioners not to cooperate with the Germans in any way. The Danish police served the escape networks rather than the German authorities.[29]

Both the warning and unified social defense enabled the great majority of Jews in Denmark to find sanctuary in Sweden; only 6 percent (475 of the 7,695 Jews and family members at risk) were seized.

This seeming paradox emerges: that collective behavior that is not considered altruism by the actors—Danish Jews were to other Danes Jewish Danes, that is, *one of us*—has become an exemplary case of collective altruism. But were one to find the victim or beneficiary defined as such in other cases labeled as altruism, this might not be a paradox but would appear to be a prerequisite or necessary condition for collective altruism.

Reserving judgment about labeling their behavior, one must look at the critical variables accounting for the response of the Danes. First, the victim was defined as "one of us" before the emergency; the violation of the rights of one was seen by all as a violation of all. Second, there was a consensus of religious and secular authorities that the German action to deport the Jews must be resisted. Third, the threat and obligation to respond was communicated immediately. Fourth, preexistent organization and social networks—schools, hospitals, rings of professionals, political party organizations, and so on—articulated and reinforced the rule of the day that the prime duty of every Dane was to help the Jews escape to Sweden; and fifth, their resources and command of their members' time were exploited for this purpose. Last (not described herein), social control was exerted to diminish the likelihood of anyone informing the German authorities of what was going on (which they knew anyway) and thus provoking the occupiers to suppress rescue activities and catch the Jews. One does not know whether to attribute the way German officers "overlooked" the operation to the rivalry between the German Army and the Gestapo, the Germans' fear of increasing their isolation from the Danes or of provoking mass disturbances they could not quell or whether the Danish context might have enabled some to act out beliefs opposed to Nazi persecution of the Jews that they might have repressed in other contexts.

Less well known are the rescue activities of the French Huguenot commune of Le Chambon sur Lignon commemorated by Phillip Hallie, whose exposition I have relied on.[30] In the case of Le Chambon, an isolated mountain village, Jews were known before World War II mostly as summer visitors. It was the pastor of Le Chambon, André Trocmé, who defined the Jewish refugees interned in French camps (by acts of prewar French governments and Vichy) and foreign-born Jews still free but sought by French and German police as "our brothers [who] are threatened with deportation" in 1942. The French authorities in Vichy, the legally constituted government of France, in cooperation with the German authorities occupying the north of France by terms of the truce ending their conflict, mandated their deportation. Most of those in danger then were not French citizens, and many could not speak French.

The Trocmés first became aware of the refugees' desperation when some knocked at their door, asking the family's help in securing new identification papers that did not mark them as "juifs." Trocmé sought out a representative of the American Friends Service Committee, which helped Jewish children get out of the camps, exploiting legal loopholes. He agreed to harbor Jewish children in the village, in his home, and in those of his parishioners with the approval of his presbytery council. His interpretation of the Gospel, reiterating the implication of the parable of the Good Samaritan that one's neighbor is the one who is in need here and now, was communicated to his congregation directly through his sermons and indirectly through the *responsables*, thirteen leaders of youth groups within the parish who conveyed his messages and directives regularly to all congregants. These leaders—teachers, instigators, enthusiasts, and organizers—were the key to the social defense network established in Le Chambon, which is estimated to have saved 2,500 Jewish refugees.

Their defense brought the commune into conflict with the Vichy authorities (and after the German occupation of the unoccupied zone with the German police) and with the head of the Reformed Church in France, who feared that Trocmé's defiance would provoke reprisals against the church. Their actions in defense of the Jews instigated internal conflict in the Trocmés (and others in Le Chambon) because it was against their faith to lie or dissimulate, but they had to in order to save lives. Trocmé frankly admitted that he was aiding Jews but refused to identify them.

The unified defense of the Jews by the Huguenots of Le Chambon could be related to their historic consciousness of themselves as an oppressed minority. However, the traditions of minorities do not in themselves cause people to react to the victims of their day in such a way as they would like their ancestors to have been treated.

What happened at Le Chambon was not replicated in any other Protestant commune in France. The Huguenots' transformation of Le Chambon into a village of refuge was a collective enactment of their transhistorical ideal of community, fulfilling the Mosaic injunction to establish cities of refuge to protect the innocent from vengeful assailants "lest innocent blood be shed" (Deut. 19:7–10). André Trocmé drew upon this tradition, instigating and leading his parishioners to defy the state, using the network of *résponsables* (which he had established to evoke wider participation in the spiritual quest of the church) as the basis of a social defense network to save Jews who sought out Le Chambon as an island of refuge. His leadership defined the threat against the Jews as a crisis and persuaded the governing authority of his church. They were united against French secular authority, whereas in Denmark, both Danish secular and religious authorities were on the side of the Jews. The threat was recognized, communicated, and acted upon immediately. In fact, involvement with the stigmatized Jews began before the gravest threat—of deportation—was presented. Communication had to be on the basis of an earlier understanding; for when the refugees arrived needing assistance immediately—housing, identity papers, ration cards, food—discretion was a necessity to protect the operation. To save lives, one had to act in terms of a situational ethic that overruled the injunction not to bear false witness at times.

The risks of their action were higher for the people of Le Chambon than for the Danes because their defense of the Jews in Le Chambon brought them into conflict with the German and the French police, whereas in Denmark all Danish authorities backed the defense of the Jews, and German officials often overlooked the movement unfolding in front of them. The church and commune of Le Chambon had no sanctions apart from collective public opinion to deter informers. Yet the people of Le Chambon who stood against the state as a minority on behalf of another minority did not consider their behavior an act of altruism or heroism but a simple duty. Their most usual account of their behavior in retrospect was, "Well, where else could they go? I had to take them in."[31]

Less well documented instances of collective hiding of Jewish evaders by a Baptist village in Poland (and by other groups there) have also been reported despite the Germans' widespread use of the death penalty there and collective reprisals against Poles for any infraction of German rules.[32] But aid to Jews in hiding was a more deviant response in Poland than in occupied western Europe not only because of the greater threat of violent German reprisals but because of the division among Poles on defense of the Jews, leading some elements in the national resistance to support such aid and other organized forces to counsel betrayal.[33]

In the cases of Denmark and Le Chambon, the focus is on collectivities—in one case, the community comprising the nation, and in the other, a religious minority in the nation composing the majority of the commune—taking risks and conspiring against the authorities to defend a persecuted minority. One might call it collective altruism if Jews are classified as the other, as they have usually been in western civilization. But to both the Danes and the people of Le Chambon it was a case of self-defense of their collective identity: for the Danes, it was a defense of their national integrity, while for the Huguenots of Le Chambon, it was a defense of their symbolic identity as it had been situationally defined. Thus, both denied that Jews were "the other."

The Indochinese Refugee Crisis and U. S. Response in 1979

The question of helping strangers—strangers who were several thousand miles away but visible on television sets in the United States—again emerged in 1978–79 during the Indochinese refugee crisis. The crisis, which meant to the nations of first asylum in southeast Asia an accumulation of hundreds of thousands of people landing on their shores with no place to go, had been growing during 1978. When the *Hai Hong* arrived in October 1978 first in Indonesia, then in Singapore, with over 2,000 Vietnamese on board, it began to be recognized as an outcome of Vietnamese-government expulsion rather than the spontaneous and covert flight of refugees in small boats (which had occurred since 1975). The actions of Vietnam that pressed the ethnic Chinese to flee and then fleeced them—demanding payment in gold for their exodus—also enabled other Vietnamese to leave illicitly.[34] The nations of first asylum—Hong Kong, Indonesia, Malaysia, the Philippines, Singapore, Thailand, and Taiwan—who reluctantly accepted 14,000 refugees in December 1978 soon found themselves confronted by a rapidly increasing exodus that reached 57,000 in June 1979 alone.

The arriving boat people were estimated to be about half or less of those leaving Vietnam—the survivors of the stormy South China Sea, thirst, piracy, leaky boats, and the failure of commercial ships and tankers to rescue them. Besides the boat people, there were Laotian and Hmong refugees threatened with death by the new government of Laos, and Kampucheans regarded as "illegal immigrants" threatened with starvation who fled to Thailand. Over a quarter-million land and boat people were interned in camps in south Asia by June 1979 with virtually no place to go.

The nations of first asylum feared having to take in the refugees permanently or being stuck with a large residue, apprehending that it would alter their prospects for economic development, change their ethnic balance, and elicit a domestic backlash from opposition parties and their constituencies. Singapore consistently refused to admit any refugees who did not have a promise of readmission elsewhere. They pressed the west and the United Nations High Commissioner of Refugees to find a solution, but the UN did not, it became apparent, after the Geneva Conference of December 1978 produce anything much: while there were commitments to take in 82,350 Indochinese refugees over a one-year span, there were about 200,000 then in camps and more arriving each day.

In January 1979, Malaysia banned the entry of new boat people, but could not consistently enforce its decree. An unknown number of boat people died after reaching Malaysian shores, being turned back in leaky craft, or in one case towed out to sea while picking up water and cut off by a Malaysian Navy boat, which caused the death of 115 refugees. By June 1979, Malaysia's deputy prime minister was quoted in the press as saying Malaysia would pass legislation to shoot refugees attempting to enter Malaysian waters on sight and ship those in camps back to sea; other nations of first asylum soon thereafter threatened to ban or enforce their ban against the entry of refugees. Thailand began to repatriate newer Kampuchean arrivals, forcibly ejecting them over a mine-strewn border where they might be shot on sight.[35]

To many, the situation in southeast Asia recalled pre-Holocaust Germany, which openly declared its aim of ridding itself of its Jews, and evoked the Holocaust in that the boat people and other refugees might be considered victims of latent genocide—caused to die by state actions and inactions—a surplus people consigned to the waves. Singapore's foreign minister, S. Rajaratnam, compared Vietnam's expulsion to Hitler's Final Solution, the open sea being "a poor man's alternative to the gas chamber."[36] He and others ASEAN members saw it as both a policy of genocide and aggression against neighboring states by "population bombing." The London *Economist* compared Kampucheans returned for "resettlement" to "the Jews being led to the showers" (21 July 1979). Others recalled that the Jews of Germany were the first "boat people," recalling how the *St. Louis*, a German luxury ship filled with Jewish refugees who had been initially promised asylum in Cuba, was turned away from Cuba and the United States in 1939 and returned to Europe; its passengers (after several had committed or attempted suicide) were finally accepted by Great Britain, France, Belgium, and the Netherlands.[37] Few recalled the more pertinent analogy—how Great Britain had prohibited and suppressed illegal Jewish immigration from Nazi-controlled Europe through the Balkans to Palestine in 1940, leading directly to the deaths of Jews on two ships that sank and indirectly to the deaths of an unknown number of others who might have escaped but were deterred by British policy.[38]

While the circumstances provoking Vietnam to expel the Hoa (Vietnamese of Chinese ethnic origin) were not analogous to the ideological drive of Nazi Germany to exile the Jews of Germany—no Jewish state threatcned the Third Reich—the Asian reaction to the refugees was similar to the European and American reaction to Jewish refugees during the 1930s. The nations of first asylum had begun talking about their "Chinese problem"—that is, the problem supposedly created by their citizens of ethnic Chinese ancestry—as states of influx in the 1930s had talked about their Jewish problem. Talk of ousting other minority groups was also bruited about. In Malaysia, "a rather sick joke made the rounds among non-Malay, 'Got your boat ready?' they liked to ask each other."[39] Government officials in the states of first asylum expressed fear of Communist infiltrators among the refugees undermining their security, although most of the Hoa were of bourgeois origin and apolitical; similarly, Anglo-American bureaucrats had expressed fear of Nazi infiltration among Jewish refugees. To be sure, the Thai fears were better grounded, for they took in the Khmer Rouge troops of the defunct regime fleeing from the new government imposed by Vietnam. Although the expenses of refugees were borne by the United Nations High Commissioner of Refugees and not the nations of first asylum, and the expenditures in local markets brought money to the latter, the refugees were blamed for the black market, inflation, and shortages and stimulated invidious self-comparisons among poorer natives in different countries. Opposition parties in several states fomented and exploited hostility toward the refugees to attack the government. Similarly, black markets, shortages, and unemployment were blamed on the Jewish refugees in the late 1930s. There were also comparisons between the allegedly distinctive role played by the Hoa and the German Jews as a middleman-minority (usually exaggerating both cases) and how their ethnic cohesiveness and visibility drew hostility; some comparisons were apt, some inapt, some aimed at understanding and others aimed at blaming the victims.

International reaction to the pleas of the nations of first asylum before the threats of June 1979 was mainly rhetorical. The conference convened by UNHCR in December 1978 had produced few new pledges, no state taking the leadership to redress the problems of these nations. A request to the United States to build a reprocessing center in the Pacific to hold U.S.-bound refugees was rejected by U.S. representatives.

During the spring of 1979 the Carter administration did appoint a U.S. coordinator for refugee affairs and announced an increase in the Indochinese refugees to be admitted under the attorney-general's parole authority to 7,000 per month. A coalition of civil leaders and organizations serving refugees organized by the International Rescue Committee as the Citizens Committee on Indochinese Refugees that toured Southeast Asia called on the administration to double its pledge and elicited support among labor, the major religious federations, black leaders, and Congress. Eli Wiesel, chairman of the U.S. Holocaust Commission, condemned refugee quotas, which were equivalent to death certificates, and called on the administration "to learn from the history of the Holocaust not to err again."[40] These appeals, the threats from the nations of first asylum, and perhaps the visceral unrest created by the visibility of the victims prompted President Carter in late June 1979 to increase the number of Indochinese refugees the United States would accept to 14,000 a month for a year. Canada tripled its commitment.

At the UN conference in Geneva in July 1979, U.S. vice-president Walter Mondale recalled with shame the failure of the Evian conference of 1938, which made no provision to take in the German Jews. The conference was successful in instigating western Europe and Australia to accept more Indochinese refugees and persuading Vietnam, which previously had denied all responsibility for the exodus, to halt the flow and agree to an "orderly departure" of people who wished to leave. It had succeeded beyond its organizers' expectations: the commitments made increased the 125,000 resettlement places pledged by 1 June to 260,000 by 21 July 1979.

Thus there were significant differences in the generalized apprehension of the threat confronting the Indochinese refugees of 1978–79 compared to the western response to the threat confronting Jewish refugees in 1938–39. To be sure, the boat people were in imminent danger of mass death at sea in 1978–79, whereas the Jews were not in peril of mass death until 1941. Yet Hitler had alluded to the annihilation of the Jews in speeches as early as 1922, proclaimed they were the source of all evil in *Mein Kampf* in 1924, and "prophecied" in January 1939 that they would be destroyed if a second world war began: the threat was not generally recognized as a warning, however. Nor did he announce or acknowledge "the Final Solution" publicly. But there was ample evidence that Jews' lives were in danger in the German Reich, evidence freely reported by western reporters in Germany. Further, there was mass flight in 1938. It was the widespread efforts of German Jews to flee that instigated Switzerland to ask Germany to identify them, leading to the "J" on passports of German Jews, which served as another disabling stigma.[41]

Was the greater apprehension of threat to the Asian refugees of 1978–79 than to the Jews in 1938–39 explained by the greater visibility of the boat people? The relative space devoted by the media to both sets of refugees would be an index of greater visibility. Concentrating on the press, I found that contrary to my expectations, there was not more space dedicated to the Asian refugees of 1978–79 than to the Jews of 1938–39 if *New York Times* coverage is the criterion; there was substantively more news of the plight of the Jews in 1938–39 than of the Indochinese in 1978–79.[42] Since there was not mass television ownership in 1938–39, one cannot compare the extent of visual imagery.

Perhaps it was not the visibility of the victims but the frame of reference that had changed. The Holocaust had become the frame of reference setting forth expectations, consequences, and guilt-ridden memories. What counted finally was not the correctness of the comparison but the perception that the Indochinese refugee crisis, like the Jewish refugee crisis of 1938–39, was a man-made disaster in which the bystander had been or would be in complicity with the persecutor for failing to aid the victims now. Thus the memory of the Holocaust sensitized journalists, political leaders, and the conscience constituency to act now to avoid another catastrophe. The Holocaust was a signal and a portent, the bell tolling in the immediate past to remind the bystanders that "no man is an island, . . . any man's death diminishes me, because I am involved in Mankind: And therefore never send to know for whom the bell tolls; It tolls for thee."[43]

The turn in the crisis was largely due to U.S. actions, which influenced other states directly and indirectly. But President Carter's action did not reflect American majority public opinion. In August 1979, with 362,219 Indochinese existing in limbo in makeshift camps throughout Southeast Asia, a Gallup poll asked a sample of Americans: "Thinking now about the Indochinese refugees, the so-called 'boat people,' would you favor or oppose the United States relaxing its immigration policies so that many of these people could come to live in the U.S.?" The majority (57 percent) opposed it, but a sizeable minority (32 percent) favored it. The majority in every income bracket and a plurality in every educational stratum opposed it. Their response in 1979 was similar to the reaction evoked by Gallup in May 1975 when a majority (52 percent) also opposed U.S. resettlement of the Vietnamese who had fled from the new regime and a minority (36 percent) favored it.[44] At the same time, more respondents in August 1979 said they would like to see some of the refugees come to live in their community than would not welcome them.[45] That poll was taken almost two months after President Carter doubled the number of Indochinese refugees the United States would admit. Similarly, the majority polled in July 1979 in a *New York Times*/CBS News poll opposed that action by almost two to one (62 percent to 34 percent), but 60 percent replied positively when asked: "If some of these refugees settled near where you live, do you think they would be welcomed, or not really welcomed?"[46]

Did this discrepancy simply indicate a lack of reflection or interest on the part of the people responding to a question that had not really been on their mind until posed by the interviewer? Although one can explain apparent inconsistency in many ways, one can also infer from it an important clue to public responses. Americans who would resist in principle incurring any social costs attached to the immigration and resettlement of Vietnamese refugees as a category were open toward them as potential neighbors once the question of taking them in was closed.

While refugee resettlement in some nations is wholly a government responsibility performed by officials and professionals, in the United States citizens as well as voluntary organizations and the state have distinctive roles; the system "tests," in a sense, the openness of communities toward strangers, for under U.S. law, all refugees legally admitted must have sponsors. The sponsor, while not legally responsible for their maintenance, is expected to enable them to find a job, learn English, secure whatever assistance is needed, and find and furnish housing in the community. The sponsor may be an organization (including the refugee resettlement agencies' branches in the community), a private individual (an unrelated person or a relative), an employer, or a group. The group sponsors have usually been congregations or interfaith committees based on congregations in the United States, although there is no intrinsic reason that other groups could not sponsor or *ad hoc* groups could not be formed for this purpose.[47] These small groups were responsible for redefining the situation for their neighbors so that it was no longer a question of accepting an abstract other differentiated from them by language, religion, race, culture, and history—another to whom they had no links and who reminded them of a war embittering advocates and opponents.[48] Thus it became a specific question of responding to a particular person or family here and now.

The appeal to U.S. congregations provides an opportunity to examine how collective altruism or neighboring the homeless stranger is inspired and mobilized, focusing on congregations as collectivities based on common values and traditions. To be sure, refugee sponsorship implied little risk (and none comparable to the risks of lifesaving described heretofore), but it did imply costs. And to many churchgoers, it was a new challenge. They were enjoined and accustomed to helping their neighbors, but very often it was their immediate neighbor who was served by their visitations, their Christmas baskets and gifts of food, their Meals on Wheels. One may assume that the same division toward taking in Indochinese refugees discovered in national polls also existed in the churches, with either a majority or sizeable minority initially opposed to their entry. Now they were being asked to take in people whom most had never seen, with whom they often had no language in common—people who might be temporary sojourners and who could not be expected to come to their aid as might their neighbors.

I will focus on congregational sponsorship in one U.S. county to explore, first (chapter 3), the process of commitment to sponsor in terms of a preliminary model of mobilization inferred from the research previously discussed.

3

Becoming Sponsors:
From Commitment to Mobilization

EXPLORING congregational sponsorship offers an opportunity to derive "grounded theory" as to how collective altruism is mobilized outside of an emergency.[1] While the Indochinese crisis was an emergency in southeast Asia, sponsors were only asked to commit themselves toward those refugees who had achieved temporary sanctuary or been rescued. To be sure, the connection was often repeated between sponsoring the rescued and rescuing those adrift, but potential sponsors might focus on the need to take people out of the camps, to find a new home.

Three levels of U.S. response can be discerned in the Indochinese crisis. First, leadership was mobilized on the national (and international) level to take in the refugees and to guarantee their exodus from the nations of first asylum. An intermediate organizational level of leadership communicated news of the crisis to its local leaders and branches, reiterating the need to respond on a local level. In this chapter, I will concentrate on the response on the third level of local congregational leaders.

By extracting findings and commonalities from the research on altruism reviewed in chapter 1, the evidence in chapter 2, and theories of social movements, one can infer some necessary preconditions for local congregations to become sponsors. (For the reader's convenience, key terms in the following propositions are italicized.) There are three prerequisite conditions or processes needed for a group to commit itself to sponsor refugees. The first relates to the perception, definition, and *recognition* of the refugees by the potential sponsors as individuals; the second relates to the *acknowledgment* by the sponsors of their responsibility individually and collectively; and the third relates to the *organization* of that group or collectivity.

1a. The refugees must be seen or be made visible and apprehended as being in trouble. (There is agreement of theorists on this prerequisite.) Further, they must be defined as *innocent victims*—not to be blamed for their trouble—whose plight is the outcome of actions of others. The tendency to blame the victim stems from the need of onlookers to believe in a "just world."

> According to Lerner . . . , people find the suffering of innocent people—those who have done nothing to bring about their own suffering—unacceptable. Witnesses reason that if innocent people can suffer, they themselves can suffer without cause. To defend themselves from this possibility they have to engage in a defensive psychological act; if they cannot attribute the cause of others' suffering to their actions, they must attribute it to their character. Thus, the innocent victims will be negatively evaluated, devalued, so the observers' belief in a just world can be maintained.[2]

Experimental evidence indicates that victims who are seen as partly responsible for their suffering are most apt to be devalued.[3] This implies that to sustain identification with the victim and inhibit devaluation, responsibility for their plight must be attributed to others.

1b. The refugees must be defined within a common *universe of obligation* shared by members. If they are members of the same national or ethnic group, they may be perceived as symbolic kin. If they are strangers, the potential sponsors must see them as members of a universal family or global universe of obligation. (There is general agreement that identification, "we-ness," empathy, and affirmation of norms of obligation are positively related to helping.)

The following steps explain the mobilization of help, viewing congregational sponsorship as an example of a social movement within a formal organization—church or synagogue—which is characterized by a division of labor and commitment. I adopt the "resource-mobilization" approach, which relates the growth of movements to the impact of movement-entrepreneurs, organization, and structure to congregations that are organizations led by professional, formally selected moral leaders—the clergy—and informal, self-selected leaders who serve as moral entrepreneurs within the congregation.[4]

2. Potential leaders must be shown that their collective action can relieve the distress of the refugees by giving them a new home. The *acknowledgment* of responsibility to sponsor by a group or congregation

then depends on *mobilization by group leaders*, who then call upon members for support by *appeal to preexisting values and norms*.

3. Once committed, the *organization* of sponsorship draws upon existing *informal social networks* and the *formal organization* of the congregation, both relying on voluntarism and eliciting *preexistent patterns of response* to calls for help. One would expect that voluntary support of sponsorship would snowball within the church after commitment is approved and the *norm of helpfulness* for congregationally sponsored projects is evoked. Further, the *resources* of the congregation—lines of communication, funds, time, staff—can be drawn upon.

Questions begin with how the refugees were defined, and responsibility was acknowledged toward them. (1) What was the impact of national and local leadership in instigating sponsorship? Did clergy or laity take the lead? (2) How were sponsorships started? How did the question get on the congregational agenda, and how was it processed? (3) Did leaders reflect or create a popular consensus of support for sponsorship? Was the division in public opinion toward refugees shown in the polls demonstrated overtly or covertly within the congregations considering sponsorship? (4) What kinds of members (other than clergy) become leaders? How were they involved in congregations and communities in general? (5) What factors were taken into account in decision making? Did the people involve collectively weigh the costs and rewards involved in helping the strangers, or was the victims' need visible and direct enough to arouse people to direct action without calculation? (6) What other models, organizations, or instigators outside their own congregation influenced congregations to sponsor?

To explore these questions, I first draw upon my own experience as a participant-observer in sponsorship development. From September 1979 to August 1980, I was employed as director of the Indochinese Refugee Sponsorship Development Project of an organization one might call the Riverside Interfaith Council in Riverside County (pseudonymous) in the northeast United States. The project was chiefly funded by a year grant from one of the church-based voluntary agencies involved in refugee resettlement; these will be referred to hereafter as *Volags*—their own self-label—for brevity.

The Volags include denominationally affiliated organizations—Church World Service (National Council of Churches), Hebrew Immigrant Aid Society, Lutheran Immigration and Refugee Service (Lutheran Council), U.S. Catholic Conference, World Relief Refugee Services (National Association of Evangelicals)—and nonsectarian organizations such as the American Council for Nationalities Services, American Fund for Czechoslovak Refugees, the International Rescue Committee, and the Tolstoy Foundation.

In this role, I spoke before congregations and community groups to instigate sponsorships, informed and counseled sponsors, wrote recruitment and orientation material, arranged conferences and gathered information on local resources, generated publicity, and responded to questions about the refugees. At the same time, I instigated and led a community-wide interfaith sponsorship in a nearby county in which I lived (which differed materially from Riverside County), so I observed and experienced the range of emotions and problems involved in sponsorship and was seen by other sponsors as a coparticipant in the movement rather than a detached "expert." In addition to knowledge and insights acquired directly, my appreciation of the national situation was augmented by attending conferences of the Volag supporting this project and by a continuous supply of press clippings from newspapers throughout the country that this Volag forwarded to its sponsorship developers. I learned more from informal conversations at conferences with sponsorship developers throughout the nation. Six months after this position ended (winter of 1981), I interviewed for this study a systematic sample of twenty-one leaders of fourteen sponsoring committees in Riverside County. Interviews were open-ended but based on a structured questionnaire (see Appendix), usually ranged from two to four hours, and were most often conducted in the home of the interviewee and tape-recorded. The sample was systematically selected after assigning all sponsors numbers so as to obtain at least half of the community-wide, two-church, and single-congregation committees that had made a commitment to sponsorship from January 1979 to June 1980 by picking odd or even numbers. I also interviewed four other persons in Riverside County who had participated in aspects of the sponsorship that needed more assessment and national and regional representatives of the principal congregationally base Volags in 1981 for this study. Individuals, churches and organizations described or quoted herein are identified by pseudonyms, as in the rule in social science research. The sample included three of five interfaith sponsorships, two of the three joint church sponsorships, and nine of the twenty single-congregation sponsorships in that period.[5] The nine congregations and the two joint sponsorships included four Roman Catholic churches and six Protestant and two other Christian congregations. The twenty-eight committees from which the sample was drawn included five Roman Catholic churches and twenty-one Protestant and two other Christian congregations and five interfaith committees. The overrepresentation of Roman Catholic churches (by chance) proved to be an asset in analysis, for it enabled me to observe differences between Roman Catholic and other churches on occasion. Since I had interviewed leaders of several other committees when I assumed the position (in order to learn) and had talked extensively over the phone with many other committee leaders—

both in congregations included and others excluded from the sample—I knew how most of the committees functioned and appreciated the range and typicality of problems presented before I began.

Both participant-observation and interviewing are independent methods, but each conditioned the uses of the other in this instance. Participant-observation is a classic method of obtaining insight into a group or social organization in which one is an outsider, enabling the observer to elicit, understand, and intuit the views and acts of group members that would otherwise be not discussed, masked, or not talked about. My respondents may have been freer in expressing exasperation and anger about sponsorship experiences in talking to me than with another interviewer because they knew I had shared the same experience and commitment.

Yet the participant-observer who plays a special part may have less access or rapport with other potential informants because of the role that person plays. In this case, data are lacking to compare leaders in sponsoring churches with members of those churches and to compare both with leaders and members of nonsponsoring churches (except in terms of denominational and Riverside Interfaith Council affiliation) both because (1) there was no source of systematic data on characteristics of church members, leaders, and/or churches in the county, and (2) I did not think it would be productive to interview leaders (laity and clergy) of nonsponsoring congregations as to why they did not sponsor, nor would it be correct to mask the purpose of my research and interview them under a pretense. Because I was well known as director of the refugee project—a salaried advocate of sponsorship—I believed it unlikely that I'd elicit anything more than I'd already been told by them.

Leaders interviewed either played the role of *mobilizers* who started committees and generated support for commitment within their congregation and/or *coordinators* or chairpersons who led the sponsorship. Nine committees had sponsored one family, and one interfaith committee sponsored no one as it disbanded before arrival of the refugees whose sponsorship was taken over by a church on the committee.[6] From 1 March 1979 to 31 December 1980, 158 Indochinese refugees sponsored by such committees arrived in Riverside County. Adding these to the previously resident Indochinese population, there was about one Indochinese to every thousand persons in the county in 1980.

No attempt is made herein to generalize findings to a population of sponsors larger than those in Riverside County because there is no demographic data collected about the population of sponsorship leaders or sponsoring groups and/or sponsoring churches that would allow me to test the representativeness of the leadership sample or compare its similarities to a national sample. However, I have no reason to believe it is not representative. Further, the motives expressed and interactions and problems observed were similar to those in other sponsorship groups, which other sponsorship developers in different regions spoke and wrote about.

History and Context of Sponsorship in the County

Riverside County is a historic site of pre-Revolutionary settlement that has moved from large estates to agriculture to industry as the basis of economic development over three centuries. Its bucolic vistas of river, hills, meadows, and brooks with eighteenth-century Indian place-names and its historic homes and mansions will hardly be seen by the casual visitor driving through its principal artery (paralleling the river), which is lined with shopping centers, industrial plants, and suburban developments. Its population (growing for four decades) of 245,000 in 1980 was formally distributed in several small cities (the largest of which was around 30,000)[7] and villages of 2,000 to 10,000, but the more concentrated western strip (which contains the government and most industry and schools) paralleling the river is actually an urban-suburban band with continuous suburban sprawl from twentieth-century growth linking the older sites of settlement. As one moves north and east, settlement is more strung out as commuting time to the locus of activity in the county increases and land is less suitable for development.

Its work force in 1980 was diversified and predominantly urban: 34 percent were professionals, managerial, or technical workers and administrators; 24 percent were sales and clerical workers; 25 percent were blue-collar workers; 15 percent were service workers; only 2 percent (farmers and farm laborers) were in agriculture. Much of the growth in the county may be attributable to the expansion of a major information-processing company, which I shall call Information Across the World (IAW). Riverside County is also within the exurban zone (75 to 150 miles) of several major eastern metropolises and has convenient and frequent rail service to the closest one, but its economy is not that of a bedroom community. It is one of the most prosperous developing areas of the state, and while not immune from national economic trends, it has not been seriously injured by the problems of deindustrialization of the northeast because of its economic mix. About the time the sponsorship project began (June 1979), the unemployment rate was almost half the rate of the state in which Riverside County is located and less than the national rate; although it rose by 60 percent in six months (as unemployment rose state and nationwide), it was still substantively lower than that of the nation in January 1980.

Preliminary census figures show that the county is rather homogeneous.

In 1980, 90.8 percent of the population was white, 6.9 percent was black, a
nd 1.2 percent was of Asian origin. (The remainder is of North American
nonwhite and other origin.) Apart from the black community (about
17,000), the largest minority was the almost 6,000 persons of Spanish
origin who constituted 2.5 percent of the 1980 population. There is also an
organized Chinese community and Asian—Indian, Chinese, Korean, and
Muslim—and European—Greek, Hungarian, Italian, and Polish—congregations. Most of the Asian-Ameicans are well educated, and many may
have settled in Riverside County because of their employment with IAW,
as have Asian and western European nationals here for a temporary stay.
The 1980 census of Riverside County shows direct evidence of the former;
almost two out of three Asian-Americans (65.6 percent) over 25 years of
age have four years or more of college, in contrast to almost one of five
whites (19.2 percent) and less than one in ten blacks (7.8 percent) in this
age category.

The Riverside Interfaith Council has been in existence since 1972 and
comprised 87 congregations, or 43 percent of the 201 churches, synagogues, and religious groups in Riverside County in 1979. Most of its
members belong to the long-established "main-line" denominations: the
evangelicals maintain a separate organization. Many occasions for interfaith cooperation punctuate the year: music festivals, thanksgiving services, hunger walks, and convocations bringing members of different
faiths together for social action, dialogue, worship, and sociability. The
RIC and the Red Cross convened an interfaith task force in 1975 to take
over the sponsorship of Vietnamese refugees who had been sponsored en
masse by a local manufacturer. Complaints and resignations indicated that
the sponsorship had broken down, and both the workers and employer
were disgruntled and resentful. (The voluntary agencies involved no
longer arrange employer sponsorships because of the likelihood that they
will be unsatisfactory and exploitative.) Twenty-one congregations became
sponsors, each sustaining one family with the advice and support they
needed. In fact, many of these were individual and couple sponsorships
backed nominally by their churches and synagogues.

Eighty-one percent of the Vietnamese refugees who had arrived in
Riverside County in 1975 had left by 1979, mostly moving to sunbelt
states. However, other Vietnamese people, usually associated with IAW,
had moved in. Like other IAW technical and managerial employees, they
tended to be well educated. Besides the Vietnamese who had fled directly
after the fall of Saigon, there was a sprinkling of Vietnamese college
students, war brides, and a priest who had come within the last ten years.
Although there are no data to document this, it appeared that the Vietnamese population who stayed on or migrated to Riverside County was
well educated and/or oriented toward obtaining higher education as a

means of mobility. Besides the approximately 100 Vietnamese, there was one Lao couple known to be in Riverside County in June 1979. The husband was also with IAW.

Because of its successful experience in 1975, the RIC undertook the Indochinese Sponsorship Development Project in September 1979 after obtaining a modest grant from one of the denominationally based Volags for this purpose. The RIC had previously convened two public meetings about sponsoring in the spring of 1979 and was known as a source of sponsorship information.

The Organizational Diffusion of Sponsorship

The first question posed pertains to how the organization and affiliations of congregations are related to sponsorship. Because no synagogues in the county sponsored Indochinese refugees (they were sponsoring Soviet Jewish refugees at this time), my analysis hereafter is restricted to churches. One may inquire: Are churches on some network or affiliated with some denominations more likely to sponsor refugees than are other churches? How can this best be explained?

Assuming that organizations both reinforce and reflect the values of their constituents and communicate the need for relevant actions, one would expect that congregations affiliated with the RIC would be more likely to sponsor refugees than would other congregations. (This, in effect, is a test of the efficacy of the Indochinese Sponsorship Development Project of the RIC.) However, since congregations are also constituents of denominations with different beliefs, practical emphases, and commitments, one would expect that denominational commitments and emphases would be related to congregations' likelihood of becoming sponsors. There are many ways to classify Christian denominations for different heuristic purposes, and changing issues and religious trends related to the issue of study may also result in different categorizations. For this purpose, I have discriminated (1) main-line denominations that have espoused Christian social action in this world either directly or through federated organizations (such as the National Council of Churches) for some time, from (2) conservative and fundamentalist churches and evangelical sects that have tended to be more otherworldly in their orientation in the past (see Table 1). The classification of particular denominations (listed below Table 1) was made after discussion with the executive officer of the RIC who was most familiar with Protestant sects and denominations and with Charles Glock, a sociologist of religion who had studied religious identification for several decades. In classifying Protestant churches, I observed their self-identification through denominational membership in the National Council of Churches or the National Association of Evangelicals.

Although church federations and church-based Volags of both types have endorsed and organized sponsorships and both justify it in similar terms as a religious imperative, the evangelicals also view it as a means toward the salvation of souls. Since they are more recently organized for social action, they evoke different repertoires of response as they draw on different recollections of past activity than do main-line clergy and laity who are more accustomed to social involvement. If readiness to sponsor were positively related to past experience and repertoires, assuming a given normative commitment, one might expect main-line congregations (1) to be more likely to sponsor once again.

Table 1A compares the percentage of RIC members and nonmembers sponsoring Indochinese refugees among Christian churches in Riverside County during 1979–80 and shows that RIC members were almost four times more likely to sponsor Indochinese refugees than were nonmembers (47 percent versus 12 percent), confirming the first expectation. Table 1B compares the percentages of churches affiliated with main-line denominations sponsoring Indochinese refugees with that of other denominations sponsoring and shows that main-line denominations were almost ten times more likely to sponsor Indochinese refugees than were other denominations (39 percent versus 4 percent), confirming the second expectation. But could the greater likelihood of RIC members becoming sponsors be explained by the composition of the RIC, which is predominantly made up of main-line denominations? To test this, Table 1C compares sponsorship of main-line and other denominations by RIC membership. It shows that RIC member congregations in main-line denominations were almost twice as likely to sponsor as nonmember congregations (47 percent versus 24 percent), confirming the expectation. However, looking at the second column of Table 1C, one sees that RIC membership had virtually no impact on other churches because scarcely any of these belonged to the RIC and few among non-RIC member churches in this category sponsored.

Characteristics of the membership congregations are also related to readiness to sponsor. Black and ethnic churches (excepting a Chinese church) did not sponsor Indochinese refugees. Different reasons can be adduced for why these particular constituencies did not usually even consider refugee sponsorship.[9] Many of the Jewish synagogues who were involved in sponsoring several Soviet Jewish families during this period did consider but apparently decided against sponsorship of Indochinese refugees.

RIC membership appears to have strongly reinforced the susceptibility

Table 1

*Indochinese Refugee Sponsorship of Christian Churches in Riverside County,
1 January 1979 to 30 June 1980 by Denominational Type and Riverside Interfaith
Council Membership*

1A	RIC Members No.	%	Non-RIC Members No.	%	Total All Churches No.	%
Indochinese Refugee Sponsors	36	47%	12	12%	48	28%
Nonsponsors	42	53%	84	88%	126	72%
TOTAL	78	100%	96	100%	174	100%

1B	1 Main-line Denominations No.	%	2 Other Denominations No.	%	Total All Churches No.	%
Indochinese Refugee Sponsors	46	39%	2	4%	48	28%
Nonsponsors	72	61%	54	96%	126	72%
TOTAL	118	100%	56	100%	174	100%

1C	1 Main-line Denominations Sponsors No.	%	(No. churches in category)	2 Other Denominations Sponsors No.	%	(No. churches in category)
RIC Members	36	47%	(76)	0	—	(2)
Non-RIC Members	10	24%	(42)	2	4%	(54)

1. Includes the AME Zion Church, American Baptist Church, American Orthodox Church, Episcopal Church, Friends Meetings, Eastern Orthodox Church, Lutheran Church of America, Roman Catholic Church, Unitarian-Universalists Ass'n., United Church of Christ, United Methodist Church, United Presbyterian Church.

2. Includes Anglo-Catholic Church, Assembly of God, Conservative Baptist Ass'n., Gen. Ass'n. of Regular Baptists, Prog. National Baptist Convention, Southern Baptist Convention, The Bible Speaks, Christian and Missionary Alliance, Church of God in Christ, Church of the Nazarene, Church of Christ Scientist, Church of the Latter-Day Saints, Evangelical Friends, Plymouth Brethren, Pentecostal Churches, Seventh Day Adventists, Jehovah's Witnesses, Wesleyan Methodist Church, Lutheran Church, Mo. Synod.

Interdenominational and nondenominational churches have been excluded.

of congregations to appeals for sponsorship among main-line denominations predisposed toward sponsorship in predominantly white nonethnic churches.

The impact of denominations on a national level can be indirectly observed in Riverside County if one compares the ratio of refugees sponsored through the denominational agency through the United States to churches of that denomination across the nation and the ratio of refugees sponsored by churches of that denomination in Riverside County to the number of churches. It is an imperfect index because the national figures of refugees resettled not only include refugees sponsored by that denomination's congregations but refugees sponsored by their relatives (previous refugees) and by social-service resettlement organizations of that denomination whose entry is arranged through that denomination's resettlement Volag. Because some denominations are more likely to use congregational sponsorship than others, the national ratio does not directly compare lay involvement among denominations. Furthermore, local congregations may choose to sponsor through a Volag of another denomination or a non-denominational Volag for a number of reasons, and those sponsorships would not be reflected in their denominational Volag's figures.

Table 2 shows that high denominations nationally are high-ranking locally and that the ratio of refugees sponsored to churches in Riverside County exceeded the national ratio by 33 percent to over 300 percent in four of the five leading denominations. In fact, it is probably that the first ranking denomination's churches also exceeded national church participation had figures for that Volag been compiled on the basis of its congregational sponsorships across the nation. That Volag is noted for a high percentage of relative and caseworker sponsorships.

Instigation of Sponsorship

Potential sponsors were approached by several methods. All congregations in the county, regardless of membership in the RIC, were invited to regional meetings in a nearby church and to county-wide assemblies. At these meetings, a film about the refugee crisis and the process of sponsorship was shown; I gave a brief talk (later outlined), and often active sponsors (and sometimes 1975 refugees) spoke about their experiences and the speakers answered questions. A congregational representative might come to an RIC informational meeting and then go back to his or her congregation to test and to mobilize sentiment. On other occasions, I was invited by a representative of the congregation (the pastor or a board member) to speak informally to an interested group from their congregation or to address the whole assembly from the pulpit. The local council of ministers (ministerium) sometimes invited me to address them at a regular meeting. I also spoke before other community groups, but such contacts never produced sponsorships. Some invitations were directly solicited by me. Telephone solicitation and information mailed in response to telephone inquiries supplemented these direct contacts, but few congregations committed themselves to sponsorship without at least one meeting where all concerned could freely question me or an experienced sponsor.

Three of every five congregations that actively considered sponsorship

Table 2
*Ratio of Indochinese Refugees Resettled to Churches
in 1979 in Riverside County and United States
for Five Leading Denominations*

Denominations (ranked by no. refugees resettled by denominational Volag in 1979)	1979 No. of Indochinese refugees resettled U.S.	Ratio of Indochinese Refugees Resettled: No. of churches in denomination (Churches = 1).			
		All U.S.	Rank	Riverside County	Rank
First	43,962	2.4	1	1.5	2
Second	10,819	.65	2	1.4	3
Third	3,505	.50	3	1.7	1
Fourth	2,799	.13	5	.17	5
Fifth	2,765	.48	4	.67	4

SOURCES: Internal Volag. statistics, church yearbooks, and RIC records.

(that is, sent a representative to a meeting, invited me to speak before them, or brought up the question officially in a committee or decision-making body) sponsored refugees. The indispensable ingredient for sponsorship was at least one enthusiast who was a core member of the church, a person who led or actively participated in church governance, committees, or ongoing service functions and could mobilize a nucleus of others from such associations or attract a core from throughout the church. If an enthusiast whose own commitment did not depend on majority sentiment was lacking, there would be no sponsorship. For the majority in all congregations scarcely ever debated the question or considered it before the leadership brought it up. Leaders in churches in which there was controversy over this among core members mobilized (if ever) later in the year.

The movement was led by the clergy in one out of three sponsorships, either being proposed from the pulpit (and approved by the church governing board or the whole congregation) or sponsored by the local ministerium. Clergy-led sponsorships included two of the three interfaith sponsorships, one joint sponsorship, and two of the single-church sponsorships in the sample. The clergy actively supported sponsorship in another third of the cases, endorsing it in sermons (after support had already been mobilized by an enthusiast) and helping the committee directly. In the last third, the clergy was in the rear guard, climbing on the bandwagon or giving reluctant approval only after support developed.

Only a minority of clergy in the county were leaders in the sponsorship movement—perhaps one in six if one includes all the clergy belonging to ministeria authorizing sponsorshp as well as those giving sermons as leaders; among main-line congregations who were most likely to sponsor, one in three ministers were leaders. (Indeed, scarcely any other than main-line ministers were advocates of sponsorship.) A previous study of Protestant clergy showed that the reluctance of most ministers to preach on controversial issues can be largely explained by their emphases on otherworldliness and individual salvation.[10] The outspoken minority among the clergy in that study was accounted for by the "New Breed" of younger ministers entering the clergy who were committed to Christian witness in this world. Although sponsorship was not a controversial issue among the churches, it may be that it was perceived by some clergy to be a question that might divide the congregation.

Although few clergy espoused sponsorship prior to a swelling of support for it among leaders of their congregations, in the great majority of known cases where clergy did publicly advocate it, their congregations sponsored.

Profile of Lay Leaders

Apart from the clergy, who were the initial enthusiasts or mobilizers who put the question on the agenda of the church? A profile of mobilizers interviewed showed that most belonged to their denomination all their life, to their church for over three years (and half for over ten years), and all are active members of the church—indeed, it is often the center of their social life. By contrast, surveys conducted between 1973 and 1977 indicated that from 26 percent to 45 percent of white Protestants have switched from the denomination of their family of orientation, and switchers were more likely to be high in church attendance than stayers.[11]

They serve as at least one (and usually more than one) of the following: member of church governing body, chair of church committee (especially the mission or social action committee), leader of prayer group, Sunday-school teacher, choir member, newsletter editor, leader of men's or women's guild within the church. For most, virtually all their organizational participation is devoted to the church. Most are highly involved in the church as a community as well as an association.[12] Two out of three mobilizers say at least half or most of their friends belong to the same church. Several refer to their church as if it were an extended family.

Since mobilizers and group coordinators (who sometimes succeeded them) resemble each other in terms of demographic and socioeconomic attributes, I will describe them together and show (wherever possible) how they differ from the population of Riverside County. (It would be most desirable if one could compare them with other church members, but since there is no source on characteristics of the latter, this cannot be done.) Typically, they are well educated, married, living together, and fully employed (if male) as professionals or managers. Although only 19 percent of the population of Riverside County over 24 years of age in 1980 were college graduates, fifteen, or 71 percent of our sample, were college graduates and six held advanced degrees. Four had some collegiate-level training, and two were high school graduates.

The great majority are members of the new middle class based on education rather than property. Table 3 compares them with the population of Riverside County in 1980, using appropriate age categories found in the census as a basis for comparison whenever possible. It shows that sponsorship leaders were not only better educated, they were more likely to occupy higher-ranking occupational positions and to have been geographically mobile, coming from out-of-state. They are more likely to live in intact families with their spouses and children, too. (The great majority are between thirty and fifty-nine, and all, except the youngest person—in her twenties—and a widow, were married and living together.)

All are white and native born except for the two men who came here as political refugees from Communist states twenty-five years or more ago. Most work for organizations producing or depending on knowledge, firms in the less competitive sector of the economy or the nonprofit sector: these include IAW schools, churches, and nonprofit organizations. Although the great majority are managers or professionals, none were in independent businesses or self-employed professionals.

Although they had similar educational backgrounds, there is a striking contrast between the daily roles played by the ten men and eleven women in the sample. While all the men were fully employed (and more likely than other males to be fully employed), the women were apt to be unemployed or underemployed (and less likely to be employed than other women in the county), although most of those who were not employed did not have children or did not have children under twelve at home. Looking at it differently, one might observe an underrepresentation among working women (especially among working mothers) among sponsorship leaders. It seems plausible to suspect they were less likely to volunteer because their agendas were already overloaded by responsibilities.

The background characteristic most common among sponsorship leaders is higher education. One may ask how this is related to their commitment to or leadership in sponsorship. Several hypotheses may account for this, not neglecting the fact that such people are likely to lead all voluntary associations. Higher education may be related to empathy, interest in (as opposed to fear of) foreigners, and attentiveness to world affairs. College graduates were also the most sympathetic and least antagonistic category of the population to bringing in more Indochinese refugees to the United States in 1979 and to admitting the Vietnamese refugees in 1975 in the Gallup samples. Empathy was the one characteristic of almost every leader interviewed, shown by spontaneous remarks identifying with and understanding the refugees.

Table 3
*Characteristics of Sponsorship
Leaders Compared to the Population
of Riverside County in 1980*

	Sponsorship Leaders N = 21	County Population* N = 245,055
Percent college graduates among those over 24	71	19
Percent in labor force employed in managerial, professional, and technical positions	93	34
Percent in labor force employed by IAW	50	19
Percent of those employed fulltime in labor force employed by IAW	70	INA
Percent married and living together in household among those over 16	90	79
Percent moved to Riverside County:		
From other county in same state	19	25
From other state or abroad	62	21
Percent men in labor force among males over sixteen	100	72
Percent women in labor force among females over sixteen	36	47

*Based on 1980 census data prepared from magnetic tape by the State Department of Commerce, which was made available by the Riverside County Department of Planning.

Their empathy toward refugees also appears to be related to their common (and singularly articulate) conception of "what it means to be a Christian, a good Christian," which stressed active responsibility to people in need in this world. Four out of five talked about behavior:

> Liz Riordan: To follow the Golden Rule . . . to be toward others what I would want somebody to be towards me. . . .
>
> Irene Carlson: I think it's loving your neighbor. . . . Some neighbors are easier to love than others.
>
> Lorraine Ferante: A good Christian does not just accept people. . . . Jesus always saw how much better people could be. I think a good Christian always tries to upbuild anyone he comes into contact with.

Several women expressed their conviction that they had a special responsibility to share their talents because they had been fortunate, mentioning not only their material well-being but marital and psychological security. Liz Riordan, who volunteered to serve one day a week in her church—an inner-city parish—as coordinator of pastoral ministry, after having given up a full-time job as director of an information and referral service, said:

> I have had a superabundance of good things in my life. . . . At present I have no needs of my own but I try to meet needs that might occur in any life like loneliness and illness.

Lorraine Ferante also related her strong sense of personal responsibility and need to give of their relative good fortune—"both Mike and I were poor as children"—and her increased personal ability to assert herself in the last five years.

The sense of being fortunate and satisfied materially contrast with the fear expressed by some considering sponsorship that they will be deprived by refugees taking what belongs to them or other Americans. It is not simply that those expressing their recognition of relative affluence are financially secure—so are many of those who are antagonistic or apathetic toward involvement—but that they feel relatively enriched rather than deprived and acknowledge their responsibility toward others who are in need.

Another related conception of the good Christian expressed by a third of those interviewed was identification with Christ as a personal model:

> Bruce Gerzuny: To be a Christian is to recognize this man, Jesus Christ, as a prototype for your life. . . . I'm a Christian because he is a man I'd like to model myself after.

> George Gough: It means to reflect the Gospel of Jesus Christ in our lives . . . to feed the hungry, to take in the stranger. . . . What you do to the least of these is what you do unto me.

> Arthur Brown: It is just to try to follow the ways of Christ . . . to be Christ-like . . . to be what our Lord expects us to be.

There was no difference between the conceptions of Protestants and Roman Catholics. Men were more likely to stress personal identification with Christ as a model than were women. Linda Valentine identified with Christ in a different way:

> It means belief in Christ, following his word in our lives. We can love others because of the love Christ showed us. We help others not just out of obligation but because we don't want to disappoint Christ just as a child lives up to his parents' standards because he doesn't want to disappoint them.

What is striking is that none attributed any importance to religious dogma, churchgoing, or ritual adherence as criteria or signs of being a good Christian. It is being and giving, rather than belief and formal participation that counts to most of them.

Who had influenced them as models? Sorokin, London, and Rosenham all remarked on how common was strong identification with one or both parents as moral models among their samples best labeled by Rosenham as "autonomous altruists."[13] When asked who had influenced their readiness to act on their beliefs, only one-third of these leaders mentioned their parents. If I include other family members and teachers among childhood models, two-thirds recalled at least one childhood model. Most of the others referred to friends, colleagues, and clergy encountered as adults. Several reiterated the impact of different people influencing them in different periods.

To this point, I have assumed that their acknowledgment of personal responsibility toward the Indochinese refugees is related to their sense of universal responsibilities toward strangers, which is embedded in the Judeo-Christian tradition, and their discussion of Christian witness confirms this. But how strange is this stranger for whom these middle-class white American Christians feel responsible? While most of them had not known any people from the nations of Indochina before sponsorship, almost two out of three presently knew or had known at least one Asian in an equal-status relationship—as friend, college roommate or classmate, or business colleague. (Since Asian-Americans in Riverside County are predominantly well educated, they are likely to encounter them in equal-status relationships at work and in the community.) None expressed fears of cultural differences, and only a few worried about whether Americans would accept the refugees when committing themselves.

None had served in the armed forces during the U.S. war in Indochina, an experience that has estranged some veterans from the peoples of Indochina. Thus, none had personal grounds for any negative feeling toward the refugees, and most had neutral or positive contacts with peoples of Asian descent. All appeared to view the Indochinese refugees as innocent victims and had no negative preconceptions about them.

Apart from their common conception of what it means to be a Christian and the importance such identification seems to have in their lives and attributes shared with millions of educated middle-class Americans, these leaders cannot be typed as a group. Their differences are as important as what they hold in common.

Nor, as a personal observer, do I think that others would characterize many people in this sample as leaders in any generalized sense. While many were self-confident, felt competent, and enjoyed or are not inhibited by an audience, others were quaking inside about organization and disliked even calling strangers on the telephone. Some were stirring speakers, evoking vicarious enthusiasm; others were dry and prosaic. As experienced sponsors, even the latter were effective as models for potential sponsors, for their very ordinariness elicited trust and mobilized support, reinforcing the conviction of the potential convert that they can do what these people did.

There is little evidence that they are more likely to be political or civic activists than other citizens of the same background. Sixty-two percent belonged to one or more voluntary associations, the same percentage reported by surveys of adults in the United States in the last decade.[14] Two could be labeled civic activists, serving on local library, historical-society, and health-association boards. For the others, the engagement with their churches is their major avocational involvement. Almost all voted in the 1980 election, but that is not exceptional for citizens with the same education and occupational status.[15] About one-third could be labeled as minimal citizens, usually voting but never communicating with their representatives or acting in concert for some political objective, and another third could be labeled active citizens, usually communicating several times a year (and at least once last year) on some public issue; many of the latter had campaigned for a candidate at least once during the last ten years. One-third could not label themselves politically; half of those willing to label themselves called themselves liberals, exceeding the proportion of the public calling themselves liberals in studies in the last decade.[16] The majority of the liberals, a minority of the conservatives, and none of the moderates were active citizens. When asked about whether they felt strongly about any current public issues, the leaders interviewed mentioned the full range of issues then before the public eye, and all views were represented. The issues included budget and tax cuts, social services, abortion, equal rights for women, nuclear energy, stopping the arms race, stopping the spread of communism, and human rights in foreign policy. No one issue was mentioned by a majority.

Another indication of how leaders reflect the spectrum of American public opinion is their views on the Indochina war. All were asked:

> During the period of the U. S. involvement in the war in Indochina, did you have strong feelings one way or the other about our role there? Did they change between 1963 and 1975? Did you act on these in any way? Have your opinions changed since that time?

This can be seen not only as an indicator of whether the sponsorship movement is associated with one position on the war but also as an indicator of whether contact with refugees ejected or fleeing from the successor Communist states of Indochina has changed their beliefs on American participation in that war, as some refugees and commentators say it should.

The greatest number who took any one position were those who originally backed or were undecided about American involvement and later decided that it was a mistake, "a foolish war," or "a useless waste of lives that should be ended as soon as possible." A minority favored the U.S. involvement throughout, seeing it as an idealistic intervention motivated by a desire to protect the freedom of the Vietnamese; their only regret was that the war was not won, which they attribute to domestic political dissent that hindered its prosecution to victory. A smaller minority were opposed to the war from the beginning. Two leaders said they had no opinion on the war because they were either apolitical or too busy to have thought about it during that period. Other responses were more complex and could not be meaningfully aggregated.

If one compares only leaders who had categorical opinion as above, the range of leaders' views and self-reported changes are consistent with changes in the range and direction of American public opinion on that war between 1965 and 1973.[17] Not a single person reports changing his or her opinion since then on the basis of subsequent events in Indochina. Thus, it appears the sponsorship movement aroused enthusiasm across political lines and was consistent with a range of previous opinions.

One may ask: what moved the mobilizers among the leaders? No one but several instigators usually reinforced their enthusiasm. They most often remarked on the influence of sponsors from other churches in Riverside County whom they knew personally through their workplace or met at RIC meetings. IAW and the RIC were the organizational webs bringing most of them together. IAW has a policy of encouraging public service among its employees, and its staff newspaper did a feature story highlighting IAW employees who were sponsors. In the town closest to IAW where most of the earliest sponsors lived, six of the twelve churches either sponsored individually or jointly during this period. The local newspapers that headlined the arrival of the refugees and printed several human-interest stories on different families aroused public consciousness, as did the IAW.

While many people mentioned the national media as a source of recognition that the boat people were innocent victims, no one was instigated to sponsor by it. To my knowledge, none of the Volags used the national media to develop sponsorships.

Nine leaders (43 percent) remarked on the influence of their clergy who advocated sponsorship and/or encouraged key members of their congregation to further explore it. Protestant clergy more often delivered such sermons before the sponsorship movement developed within their congregations than did Roman Catholic clergy, who usually approved or encouraged mobilizers once support developed. Many people served as instigators, both people who were looked up to as models of moral authority (usually clergy) and other sponsors who were peer models—

people at their level with whom potential sponsors could compare themselves, from whom they could learn and anticipate enacting the role of a sponsor.

A minority of leaders had acknowledged they could and should do something to help the refugees prior to such instigation. Two of the five leaders who felt such a need had themselves been political refugees from Communist states and were moved by personal identification with the new refugees:

> Ruby Breda: Because I was a refugee, I felt the need to help other refugees to find a new land and make a new life.

> Saul Kim: I was aware of the need months before I did anything but I didn't think I was going to do anything. . . . It wasn't my job [in the church]. . . . When it became clear that the church wasn't going to do anything, I decided to do something and went and talked to the pastor.

One of the leaders who joined the movement later (1980) as a committee leader was Linda Valentine, who felt a burning need to do something in early 1979 but did not become a mobilizer:

> My husband would find me in tears every night watching television. . . . As a mother, I couldn't stand to watch children dying. I didn't know what to do . . . contributing money just wasn't enough.

This inactivity on Linda's part despite great turmoil demands attention, for Linda is a political activist who grew up in a family of professional politicians and had learned of the possibilities of church sponsorship from a fellow teacher she greatly admired. Linda did nothing, she says, because she was sure that no one in her church would be interested, a church of her husband's faith to which she had converted, and a church whose members she viewed as lacking social consciousness. After a community-wide sponsorship had been authorized in her town by the council of ministers, her husband, a delegate to that council (their church lacked a minister at the time), volunteered her services to the sponsorship committee. Within a month, she became coordinator.

By contrast, Irene Carlson, a lifelong resident of the county firmly rooted in the networks of her church (in a denomination to which she had been attached all her life), went straight ahead despite the disinterest of her pastor:

> I was very concerned—you know all we've read about the Holocaust—I just thought—I don't really want this on my conscience that people were clinging to boats and nobody came to help them. I asked again to have it put in the Bulletin.

Irene's tenacity was whetted by an unsuccessful experience in 1975 when she had persuaded her church to sponsor Vietnamese refugees, but by the time they decided there were no more refugees left to be sponsored. Her active participation in the RIC also exposed her to additional influences promoting sponsorship.

There are many differences between these two women and their situations; Linda's assessment of the probable response in her church may have been accurate. But the outstanding question is why one tried and the other did not. The differences in their responses point up the need in sponsorship development to recruit enthusiasts who are embedded in the church as a community and association and secure in the belief that others will listen to them. The two experiences with enthusiasts who were not embedded indicate they will have a hard time evoking support.

From Instigation to Authorization of Sponsorship

Once sponsorship was put on the church agenda, the movement was more likely to gather supporters if endorsed by the minister. Until a core of supporters grew (less than five were enough if no resistance emerged), it would not move up on the agenda. Organized factionalism against sponsorship was rare. Sometimes the core emerged from a prayer group, a hunger task force, or a social action committee to which the mobilizer belonged. Apart from the clergy-led sponsorships, there is usually only one mobilizer at any time who carries the project from concept to commitment, addressing the practical questions that are raised, exorcizing doubt and temporizing, spreading the word, and putting the question on the agenda.

In Protestant churches, sponsorship usually must be authorized by the governing body of the church: the Administrative Board (Methodist), the Vestry (Episcopalian), the Session (Presbyterian). Direct votes on the question by the whole congregation were infrequent. In Roman Catholic churches, the head priest of the parish had to approve the request to sponsor. (Some parishes had a lay parish council, but in none studied was it a decision-making body.) Once the priest was convinced that there was sufficient lay support so that the obligations of helping the refugees would not be imposed on the clergy, it was approved. Authorization usually occurred one to six months after the time the mobilizer first considered the idea. Churches sponsoring later in the period studied were more likely to have been internally split than churches sponsoring earlier.

After sponsorship is authorized, the original mobilizer may pass leadership over to a committee coordinator. Over half the leaders interviewed were such coordinators, coopted to take over the organizational tasks by the original mobilizers or the committee. Coordinators who were not mobilizers were less likely to be in the nuclear core of the church.

Two underlying questions are raised by church members during consideration of sponsorship that indicate how rational is their appraisal. The first set of questions is about costs and resources: What will it cost? Can we afford it? How long will the refugees be dependent on us? How will a collection fit in with our other scheduled collections? How much time will it take from our other engagements? The second question (which often underlies the first) is: "Who are these people we are being asked to help and why are we responsible for them?" The sponsorship developer or previous sponsor addressing a congregation considering sponsorship will be told that some people are saying, "Why should we help them? We have so many of our own who are unemployed, poor, needy to take care of. Why should we bring them in to take jobs away from Americans?" This will not be verbalized on the floor but be bruited informally.

The clergy may concentrate on a universalistic religious appeal. My strategy was to make both questions explicit and respond to them directly rather than to deprecate them by appeal to higher morality. Addressing the economic question first, the potential sponsor was reassured that their life-chances (and those of their neighbor) would not be diminished by the influx of a refugee family, that they could afford the costs, and they would benefit from the productivity gains and taxes contributed by these refugees, especially when they are in retirement and the refugees will still be in the labor force.

> Unemployment is rooted in maladjustments of the economic system. The idea that immigrants take away the jobs of natives rests upon the so-called "lump of labor" fallacy, namely, that "there is a limited amount of work to be done in the country, and if a stranger is allowed to nibble at the lump, there will be less of it for the native. All the economists of repute have shown this to be a fallacy." In fact, in occupying the lowest rung of the economic ladder, immigrants expand job opportunities. They impel native-born workers up the economic scale, facilitating their upward mobility, not hindering it. [18]

Potential sponsors were also reassured on this point by the support of the AFL-CIO for the Indochinese refugee program in 1979. While the above summary of the economic impact of immigration is an oversimplification, it did not misrepresent the probable effects in Riverside County. [19] One could also point out to them that each is competing on a separate track in the labor market; neither the unemployed auto worker or college professor is in competition with the refugee applying for a minimum-wage job nor are they in competition with each other. The effects of legal immigration must be discriminated from those of illegal immigration, which creates a secondary labor market in which workers without protection of the law can be readily exploited for subminimum wages.

The location of the congregation and the resources available in that region for housing, study of English as a second language, and jobs affected assessment of the costs. When churches in communities in the rural, economically depressed, and sparsely settled northern and eastern parts of the county considered sponsorship, they were more likely to reject it than were churches elsewhere. The costs and rewards of sponsorship differed appreciably in these undeveloped rural regions. Because of the lack of services, industry, and public transportation in the county, one could anticipate that small-town sponsorship in isolated villages might soon become frustrating for sponsor and refugee.

Previous commitment and experience as a sponsor also affected assessment of the costs of sponsorship. Ten, or 63 percent, of the sixteen congregations sponsoring Indochinese refugees in 1975 sponsored refugees in 1979–80. (It is not known how many of the congregations that had ever sponsored any refugees sponsored again in 1979–80; there were also congregations that had sponsored refugees from other regions previously, but there is a lack of survey data on the extent of earlier sponsorships among all congregations in the county.) The 1975 sponsors who did not sponsor again were often too well aware of the costs of sponsorship, for the individuals within their congregations most involved in 1975 sometimes had become absorbed in sustaining the refugees psychologically over several years without support from others. This "burn-out" factor, which led to the unwillingness of such people to volunteer again, and the greater proportion of women working full time were cited by several congregations sponsoring in 1975 as reasons for their present lack of interest along with organizational problems or clergy changes.

To even anticipate and assess the costs (rather than discarding them out of hand), there must be a motive to want to help the refugees. The question of acknowledging responsibility toward the stranger is basic. The following model talk, or sermon, which I devised seemed to persuade many church audiences, and related both to their values and my background and role:

The question is to whom are we obligated. Some people say we should only take care of our own—meaning the people in our own family or neighborhood or our religion or race or nation. Usually their practice is better than their principles for if someone is injured in an auto accident in front of their house, they would help them immediately without inquiring who they were, where they came from, regardless of what color they were.

The Judeo-Christian tradition has a clear answer to this question. The Bible is the story of the interaction of strangers and sojourners, people from one land who left because they were inspired by the vision of one God. They became refugees, pilgrims, slaves, liberated by a series of awesome events. . . . So we are told, "Love the sojourner therefore; for you were sojourners in the land of Egypt" (Deut. 10:18–19).

Continuing in this tradition, Jesus related the parable of the Good Samaritan to answer the question, "And who is my neighbor?" The good neighbor was not the priest or temple-goer but an outsider, the Samaritan. In this parable, we are told two things. The good neighbor may not be of your kind but he may be more worthy than priests or pious people. The good neighbor does not ask who is the injured traveler, inquiring into his religion, race or ethnic group. Neither did the Good Samaritan ask how much gold the traveler had or hospital insurance or consider whether his debt would be reimbursed. He did not form a commission on crime on the highways; he acted and did what had to be done.

The implications are clear. Ultimately, there is no we and them. . . . While in the past, the stranger or sojourner could only be conceived as one within the gates of the community who could be seen, in this global village no one is invisible unless we avert our eyes. The castoff from Indochina is visible on our nightly TV news. Were we born in the wrong place at the wrong time, we could be in the same boat.

Enthusiasts who identify with Christ as a personal model often put it in a Christological context, recalling Matthew 25:36: "I was a stranger and you took me in."

The basis for identification on religious and universalistic grounds are often supplemented by a common national identification as Americans with refugees, assuming an image of national identity celebrating the United States as a nation of refugees. One church newspaper proclaimed: "The Pilgrims were the first boat people here." Sofia Armond put it personally:

We are all refugees, after all. One of my parents was born here—the other in Canada. I'm only half-American. Of my four grandparents, none was born here.

Identification with the refugee might be reinforced by particular admiration for traits and qualities and values—hard work, respect for education, and so on. The example of 1975 refugees from Vietnam who had "made it" standing before potential sponsors seemed to inspire the respect that transforms sympathy into empathy. Thus religious, universalistic, nationalistic, and particularistic bases of identification could reinforce each other.

So far, it has been assumed that motives were other-directed, put in terms of helping the refugees, and most were, leaders referring (if pressed) to the need of the refugees for help. Only two leaders expressed their needs and expectations of the rewards as a motive:

Frank Myerhof: I was talking to some of the guys at work who were sponsoring refugees . . . it sounded like a fun thing to do.

Ellen James: I have to confess to being very selfish . . . being interested in learning about language and culture.

Once sponsorship was put on the church agenda, it was only rejected on the first ground—inadequate resources or too few members available to do the work needed. Sometimes other involvements in the community or an absence of a minister meant that all involved members had their agendas already filled. But logically, the church could not reject sponsorship on other grounds, for it could not deny obligations toward the Indochinese refugees without repudiating its own injunctions and thus producing cognitive dissonance, causing tension.[20]

Each new congregation that committed itself to sponsorship up to a certain point increased the sense that this was a social movement and became models that churches considering sponsorship could compare themselves to. Similarly, each town ministerium that sponsors is a challenge to the ministerium of the next town, which sees it as a reference model. "If Corinth and Ionia are sponsoring why aren't we doing anything in Delphi?" In one case, this provoked a ministerium to sponsor despite the frankly-voiced perception of the clergy that the town and their congregations were racist, anti-Semitic, and xenophobic. Although the idea of sponsorship raised grave misgivings and aroused more anxiety than I ever observed in a lay group, the question gave them an opportunity to cope with the dissonance generated by conflict between their ideals and the reality, to decide whether they were leaders or followers, changing prejudices or just reflecting them. The later positive response of townspeople to the refugees surprised them agreeably.

The sponsorship movement in Riverside County reached its zenith of influence in the last quarter of 1979 when a county-wide meeting drew 110 people. The RIC campaign had followed the highpoint of media coverage of the Indochinese crisis by about three months. Interest among the public and the clergy diminished in 1980 as media attention to the Indochinese situation was supplanted by crises in Afghanistan, Iran, and the Cuban refugee influx in 1980. The movement continued after the project ended (August 1980), and new refugees kept arriving, as was to be expected from the time gap between commitment, application, and arrival, but only one new sponsoring congregation was recruited in the latter half of 1980 and the mobilizer in that case first became enthused in November 1979. Reports from national representatives of the refugee Volags also showed a general decline in sponsorship interest in 1980. Thus, the project's scheduled end coincided with the national decline in commitment.

4

The Achievement of Group Sponsorship

Preparing for Sponsorship

AFTER commitment to sponsorship was authorized by the congregation(s) or the ministerium, the principal tasks of the committee preceding the arrival of the refugees were self-organization and gathering resources. New committee leaders may then have emerged who were motivated chiefly by their belief in their obligation to support church projects. These included some who originally had doubts or were not involved at all. Frank Meyerhof, for example, went to the initial meeting of people interested in sponsorship at his church, which was led by a man involved in a small prayer group (most of whom were also there), a person known for enterprise in "good works," he recalled. Frank did not sign up for any committees, expressing doubt that those people "would bring it off." But they did, and when the original mobilizer moved from the area, he asked Frank to take over the leadership. Frank bluntly said, "I'm no hero. . . . I never would have started the group myself."

Some sponsorship committees also attracted people who were not church members but wanted to help refugees directly. Interfaith and community-wide committees attracted more of them. The Canadian movement produced a nationwide network of ad hoc nonsectarian sponsorship groups, Operation Lifeline, as well as ethnic groups and congregational sponsors for over 21,000 Indochinese refugees in three months in 1979, showing that the potential for sponsorship is not limited to congregations.[1] However, in the United States all the recruitment for group sponsors has been mobilized by the denominationally affiliated Volags, and other models have not emerged.

Most of the sponsorship committees studied were organized very similarly because they had based their structure on a model derived from the successful experience of one church in 1975, which was published (in mimeograph) by the Riverside Interfaith Council as "Guidelines for Refugee Sponsorship." Each committee usually had a coordinator, treasurer, and subcommittee chair for each task area involved in resettlement: housing, transportation, furnishings and clothing, homemaking, education, medical, employment, and finance. Another structure was devised by one committee based on shared responsibility among five families who changed roles as new needs emerged. (This committee was not included in the study.) Another committee alternated the first structure with one in which responsibility for daily contact and tasks were allocated to seven women, each assigned to be "on" one day of the week. The basic RIC committee model is similar to others found in "how-to" handbooks for refugee resettlement prepared by several denominations.

Formal volunteering for specific responsibilities in advance served several functions. In the past, when one or two persons in a church had volunteered and been consigned to fill all the obligations of sponsorship without being able to count on others, that person could be wholly absorbed and drained by the role. Also, both sponsor and/or refugee might develop a need to perpetuate the dependency of the latter. Such an experience often meant that neither the sponsor nor observers of their plight were likely to volunteer again.

The alternative of dividing tasks on an ad hoc basis as they come up demands an excessive amount of time in group decision making and may lead to inequity and bad feeling: a Canadian leader described how their neighborhood group debated every step for hours at a time, yet relied on the same volunteers to execute the decisions of the group, engendering resentment.[2] The mutual commitment to the division of labor within the more structured Riverside County committees was a pledge of each to all and appeared to be accepted as just. Each subcommittee chair could recruit a committee, call up helpers as needed, put up announcements in the church bulletin for volunteers and resources, or use any other method to get help.

Were the volunteers predominantly women, as were the Canadian volunteers described by Adelman and the "good neighbors" Sorokin studied? Was sponsorship, like other "good works," relegated to women by assignment or self-selection? This would not be surprising, for traditionally such kinds of voluntarism has been viewed as a woman's role, and many churches and synagogues build these expectations into their associational structure. This was not so in Riverside County. One-fourth of the committees were made up predominantly of married couples, and another fourth had a large minority of couples. Men were more likely to head committees in Roman Catholic than in Protestant churches, and men were more likely to participate in male-headed committees than in female-headed ones.

One cannot tell from who occupied key posts who actually did what at times. One committee, which had a nominal male and female head, ended with the latter doing most of the work because the man involved just became a father and the woman was ready, willing, and able to take over. In another committee, the one committee starting with women only, several husbands became actively involved. Generally, the gender-related division of roles within committees paralleled the allocation of roles in the community. Women assumed responsibility for committees involving the home and family, while functions involved with the community—housing, transportation, jobs—were shared by men and women. The general rule, as in American society, seems to be that women can be integrated into instrumental roles outside the home, but men are not integrated into domestic roles.

Once organized, the committee's first tasks were to gather resources—money, clothes, furnishings, and sometimes contributed housing—and apply through a Volag for a family. Fund raisers were usually popularly priced events: a pot-luck dinner, a chicken barbecue, a Vietnamese dinner, or a dance. Some churches just passed the collection plate. Voluntary associations and schools also put on benefits for community-wide sponsorships. Merchants and professionals sometimes also donated services, often expecting public recognition in return but sometimes rejecting it. In several instances, substantial donations were made from the church budget itself, negating any need for fund raising. Fund raising was seldom the problem anticipated, and the funds raised—from $500 to over $3,000— often exceeded what was needed. In several instances, leaders recalled individual donors of modest means giving between $100 and $500, although there had been no appeal for large contributions: scores and sometimes hundreds contributed in some way as giving became the norm.

Besides the funds raised by the churches and the community, sponsoring committees could draw on the funds obtained through the refugee Volags who at that time received $500 per capita from the United States for each refugee resettled. From this sum, the Volags maintained their own staff (in Southeast Asia and the United States), recruited sponsors or sponsored directly, and sometimes supported related services. The Volags gave sponsors from zero to $400 per capita for each refugee sponsored;

some also give grants for special needs (medical, automobile), and others only give grants if needs that cannot be met by the sponsoring congregation are demonstrated. It appeared that the size of the grant was seldom a criteria of sponsors in choosing a Volag despite their initial anxiety about resources. Almost all chose the Volag of their denomination or the agency of a related denomination believed to most likely to process applications efficiently.

Sponsors usually decided on what kind of a household to apply for unless they were applying for a specific family known to them, which, in all likelihood, would be related to another family in the area. Most sponsors' ideal appeared to be a small nuclear family with children. The Volag called upon the sponsor to give an assurance for, or decline to accept, a particular household among those processed by the U.S. Immigration and Naturalization Service who were allocated to it by the American Council of Voluntary Agencies, the umbrella organization of the refugee Volags, at the weekly "auction" of "free cases." The committee was usually given a copy of the "biodata," a schedule compiled by interviewers representing the Volags in the camps in the nations of first asylum, which reports the refugees' name, family composition, ages, ethnicity, religion, languages spoken, nation of origin, employment history, and health as self-reported (the interviewers also appear to look at teeth), compiled by household applying for entry together. Such background on skills (sometimes, as they are in many résumés, exaggerated) may be the basis for sponsors to choose or reject a particular family. There were always jobs for auto mechanics in Riverside County, but none for fishermen. Frequently, the family offered, one of the scarce "free cases"—not previously designated to join a relative or friend in a particular region—differed from their preference. Thus, many sponsors who wanted a family with children sponsored childless couples or single young people (usually men), and virtually all sponsors of refugees arriving after April 1980 in Riverside County accepted Lao households, the Vietnamese having been absorbed by existent Vietnamese communities and the institutional sponsors in these communities.

One characteristic that Volags seldom used for matching sponsor and refugees was religion. The justifications advanced by the Volags for taking in refugees did not admit discrimination among the Indochinese refugees, and their religious and cultural diversity was accepted as a matter of course by most sponsors. Most Volags do not publicly recognize proselytism as an appropriate function of sponsorship. Several advise sponsors that refugees should not be *forced* to go to church (but they may be invited); however, some religiously based Volags have prepared materials translated into the languages of Indochina that extensively explain their faith followed by questions about it.

While waiting their arrival, the abstract refugee was fleshed out mentally by these biodata. Most sponsors in the study waited between one and three months between the time they applied and the time the refugees arrived. The length of time a sponsor waited depended on the backlog (or queue for free cases) in the Volag through which they apply, delays in processing through the U.S. Immigration and Naturalization Service, the legal category in which the principal applicant in the family falls that determines their priority, the allocation of priorities for clearing refugee camps in different nations (a political determination), last-minute "medical holds" on members of the family, and delays in transportatiion. While sponsors were usually notified within the week that the refugee household they were awaiting was scheduled for transport, frequent delays and rescheduling were the rule. Given the fact that arrangements are made several continents away through the Intergovernmental Committee on European Migration and transmitted through the Volags' West- and East-Coast offices to the sponsors, the frequency of meetings without hitches (such as refugees arriving alone in airports with no contacts there) were remarkable.

During the waiting period, the most pressing concern of most committees was housing. Sometimes a serendipitous solution was readily at hand—an apartment or house owned by the church that could be made habitable or a summer home not in use whose owners were church members that could be rented for an indefinite period at the cost of operation without paying rent in advance of arrival. The latter was important to avoid, since the family might be delayed for months and delays often could not be anticipated or explained by Volag representatives. Premature rentals cost some committees hundreds of dollars. Committees were advised to have temporary housing available in a member's home in which the refugees can stay for a week or two while the committee scours the preferred area for housing. Sponsors' choice of housing represented an attempt to maximize the interests and convenience of their members who would be working with the refugees and that of the refugees. Perfect solutions were rarely possible. Initial housing arrangements often conditioned the sponsor's and refugees' experience here in unexpected ways.

An Overview of Refugee Sponsorship as a Social Process

Before arrival of the refugees, most sponsors had time to anticipate and plan for the role (new to most) that they would play. As Van Esterik points out, this is a socially constructed and complementary role (depending on the refugees playing their part) that can be conceived of in several ways.[3] To succeed, it must go beyond complementarity toward reciprocity, beyond unilateral dependency toward equality, and become a relationship in which both parties care and are sensitive toward the other's needs. She notes that the sponsor may conceive of themselves as hosts, as adoptive parents, as teachers, or as just friends. (While Van Esterik's observations pertain to individual "in-home" sponsors, many also apply to group sponsors.) It shall be seen later how sponsors' conceptions are related to their expectations, rewards, and disappointments.

Regardless of the self-conception of sponsors, sponsorship regularly goes through similar phases. Although the end goal of sponsorship is to enable the refugee household to become autonomous and self-sufficient, the first role of the sponsor is that of a nurturer and provider: in terms of its emotional content, one perceptive pastor called this the "holding hands" phase. As the refugee becomes autonomous, the sponsor becomes a counselor and, as before, an advocate and enabler in the community when called upon. Finally, the sponsor becomes a friend and equal if the relationship proves to be enduring. Among the sponsoring committee, one or a few will develop intense bonds with the refugee, doing more for and with them than others, more than they formally committed themselves to do, and become psychically invested in them. I shall refer to them as godparents. Other core members of the committee (and peripheral members) usually accept and appreciate this, because they know they do not have the time, skill, or interest to sustain so close a relationship, understand that such a relationship cannot be routinized and is indispensable, and feel secure in their own contribution. Thus, the committee treasurer who may have only visited the refugees twice feels this is *our* family as much as the godparents.

Regardless of how one conceives one's role, the sponsor is confronted usually with the almost total dependency of the refugee, especially pronounced when the refugees cannot cope in English (which was often the case). The congregational sponsors establish the household; furnish it; provide money for food and personal needs; teach the refugee to cope with money, Food Stamps, and grocery coupons in shopping; to operate electrical stoves and appliances; to discriminate among cleaning products; to adjust heat, diet, and clothing to the weather; to get children into schools; and to get medical care as needed. Most sponsors enabled their refugees to obtain Food Stamps and Medicaid, which refugees are entitled to on the same bases as American citizens without employment or resources. (However, the entire cost for refugees in 1979–80 was borne by the federal government for the first three years after entry here.)

Essentially, it is the sponsor who determines what benefits are sought. Virtually all sponsors, regardless of denomination, opposed the use of cash assistance—nor did refugees need it as the sponsors were supporting them—but the stigma of welfare seldom extends to Medicaid or Food Stamps. Few label the latter or rent subsidies or public housing or the job-incentive program offering employers tax cuts for hiring refugees (among other targeted groups) as "welfare." The refugee is dependent on the sponsor as a surrogate in this period to apply for and obtain benefits or "entitlements." There are two unanticipated consequences of this. Middle-class sponsors with no prior experience with the welfare system often found it quixotic, frustrating, and unpredictable because of different interpretations of regulations, misinformation, or misrouting by different people. Second, refugees learned from other refugees with whom they compared themselves that they received different benefits. Later some implications of this will be examined.

Although the Volags all make clear to the sponsor that they are not legally or financially responsible for the refugee, and they may theoretically refuse to pay any debts incurred by the latter, abandon them, and cause them to seek public assistance on their own, this has never happened in my experience with congregational sponsors of Indochinese refugees nor was it mentioned by other sponsorship developers. Conversations with Volag representatives indicated that "breakdowns" in group sponsorships incur infrequently; at times they were provoked by the inappropriate expectations of sponsors (imposing work or religious obligations in exchange for hospitality) and/or refugees, and by the very location of sponsors—rural isolation especially induces strains that many refugees cannot bear. Relationships were sometimes renegotiated or sponsorships transferred by the Volags, but in other instances refugees simply left before they were self-reliant and thus were more apt to seek public assistance.

At the same time they are providers, the sponsors are agents resocializing refugees to cope with and understand American culture, enabling them to use educational services to study English as a second language (ESL), or helping them to learn English directly by tutoring them and explaining the meaning of American habits, values, culture, and conventions. Some differences of strategy exist between the government departments in the United States and among different western nations of resettlement as to the priority to be given to obtaining work immediately or sponsoring the refugees to enable them to study Survival English and to enhance their skills and potential for adaptation. Most of the Volags believe that work, usually meaning a minimum-wage job that can be filled without instruction demanding language, is the first priority to enable the refugee to become economically and psychologically self-reliant; employment, it is also said, further stimulates the refugee's need to know and motivation to learn English.

Many sponsors in Riverside County were influenced by the views of Father Paul, an articulate, urbane, trilingual Vietnamese priest who had fortuitously found himself in the United States in May 1975 and now served as counselor for scores of refugees and sponsors with problems as well as being a parish priest. Father Paul urged sponsors to enroll refugees in a full-time ESL program in the county so as to acquire minimal adequacy in English (estimated to take three to six months) before looking for a job for them. Premature job placement, he had observed, had led to dead-end jobs in which the refugee was condemned to imitate rote motions, was alienated and continually exasperated because he could not understand fellow workers and supervisors, unable either to advance and/or to express himself. Locked outside of the culture by the language barrier, the seemingly passive stranger might seethe with rage provoked by frustration and came home enervated and listless, creating family problems.

Regardless of priorities, the critical step toward independence was the employment of potential wage-earners. Occupational goals would have to be related to the refugees' background (assuming they had transferable skills that did not depend on language or accreditation), the presence of young children needing a full-time caretaker at home, and the labor market as well as the refugees' expectations and desires. Jobs usually were at the minimum-wage in services and manufacturing, did not demand literacy or written instructions, and were most often secured through personal contacts. Getting a job and forming a plan for the family's sustenance and advancement (which may involve simultaneous schooling and/or the acquisition of skills over a long period) was essential for the refugee family to become autonomous.

As the refugees become independent, the sponsors' role alters: they must surrender and accept the loss of paternalistic authority. In some cases this loss is precipitated by the refugees' departure from the area before independence is achieved, a step that is often experienced as an abrupt, wrenching, hurtful, and premature flight by godparents and other sponsors. I believe that sponsors in Riverside County were less apt to experience this as a trauma because they had been socialized to anticipate this on the basis of my descriptions of the process.[4] My counsel was based on my observation that since 81 percent of the Vietnamese refugees arriving in 1975 had departed, it was likely that many of the newer refugees would also leave. Although these sponsors were advised that sponsorship is not an adoption or contract to live in any village or county, that refugees frequently leave when they discover relatives elsewhere, and that refugees are as free to move within the United States as are American citizens, such separations were still hard to accept and mourned by some. To understand this, one must understand the nature of the social bond between sponsor and refugees, a bond transcending their functional relationship.

Most of the literature about refugee sponsorship describes it only as a formal instrumental role, in terms of its intended goals and a one-way relationship. That is, it describes what the sponsor is *supposed to do* for the refugee (not what they do) and not what the refugee does to or for the sponsor.

The informal role of the sponsor begins with indentification. Prior to arrival, the sponsor makes inferences personalizing the refugee household chosen by the committee based on their biodata, remarks about other refugees from that nation or ethnic group made by other sponsors, and general preconceptions about refugees and other Southeast Asians, some based on cultural guides published by the Volags. The first actual experience (usually restricted to the committee leaders) of meeting the refugees at arrival at the airport is often an ecstatic moment for sponsors. The sponsors are elated at that *they* have done (with minor help and sometimes interference from the U.S. government, the Volag of their choice, and several international bureaucracies) and feel fulfilled (as well as a little anxious) at meeting the real people behind the biodata. They are impressed by the seeming vulnerability of the refugees, the social sensitivity, and other charms of *their family* as they usually refer to them when not calling individual members by their first name. The sponsors' initial image of refugees conjures up the pictures of the dispossessed and hungry of the Third World advertised in the media: if their Indochinese refugees did not look like this, it was remarked upon.[5] As the refugees become real people to the sponsors and are seen as individuals, their attributes reinforce the sponsors' conviction that these are "our" people and people very much worth saving. Many sponsors have told me about their first meeting spontaneously (before the interviews for this study) and their common note of exhilaration, even elation, recalls my own experience. They later remark on how lucky they were to get this special family: "they are so bright," "such lovely people," "a family I'd choose as friends if I didn't know them," "so eager to explore and help themselves," and so forth. When such signs are not imputed, this is usually interpreted sympathetically as a product of fatigue, trauma, culture shock, fear or lack of linguistic ability. (The initial meeting is usually mediated by a translator, but the translator may not always speak or understand their dialect.)

Whatever the characteristics observed of or imputed to the refugee, the refugee-sponsor relationship creates a social bond that goes beyond the explicit or implicit contract between them. The sponsor offers protection, sustenance, and nurturance and usually elicits in return reciprocating expressions of trust, gratitude, and interest in their family from the refugees. The refugees are usually eager to respond because they, like the sponsor, have been tutored in the elemental norm of reciprocity that transcends cultures: all gifts imply a commitment, an obligation to return something to the giver. Reciprocity does not necessarily demand repayment in kind but by a good that is an equivalent pychic gratification to the recipient.[6] The sponsors feel amply rewarded by the refugees' expression of gratitude, concern, and affection. This diffuse bond of mutual concern and affection guarantees both that they will commit themselves to each other and motivates the sponsors to extend and intensify personal commitment to their role.

There is tension in a bond beginning with inequality, however, for a relationship characterized by unilateral giving and reciprocating with gratitude typifies patron-client relationships in many cultures, and patronage implies sustained dependency, manipulation, and use of the other that may provoke resentment. Sponsors are advised by the Volags and by sponsorship developers that patronage (whether materialistic, psychological, or cultural) should be avoided: sponsors should make clear to the refugees that their present inequality, their dependence upon them, is not to be permanent; they will become an independent household.

Misunderstandings inhere not only in the language barrier but in the lack of cultural equivalents known to the refugees for sponsorship (and other experiences encountered in resettlement), which might serve as models for this situation. Dr. Tran Minh Tung observes that:

> The sponsorship system . . . also leaves the refugees perplexed. They are surprised and touched by the warm and genuine concern of most sponsors since, in their country, such dedication is more likely to be directed toward one's own kin than to strangers. But if this is really generosity and saintly conduct, then one should not let it be marred by egotistical concerns and petty considerations. Actions, therefore, which, from an American's viewpoint, are only realistic and aim at fostering independence—for example, to ask the refugees to contribute to their upkeep as soon as they receive their first paycheque—often come as a shock to refugees because they are viewed as meanness and parsimony and shatter all their trust and gratitude. At any rate, ambiguity often leads to apprehension; since the refugees are not certain of how much they could expect from the sponsor, the tendency is to get out of the relationship as soon as possible.[7]

In western society, research has also shown people who are helped are more likely to have negative than positive reactions to aid when they cannot reciprocate; however, the helped may feel less indebted when they can help another as older refugees helped newer arrivals.[8] The "contract" (which should be made explicit in order to prevent ambiguity and misunderstanding) involves acceptance of both the goal of autonomy and agreement with the strategy of adaptation chosen by the sponsor. It shall be seen that a paradox appears: the contract "works" only if the social bond between sponsor and refugee is unimpaired; the bond is tested by conflict over the terms of the contract. But if the contract is conceived of by the refugee as an abridgement of the freedom he or she would have if dependent on the government, an impersonal bureaucracy, rather than a better strategy to become independent, the contract may reinforce their feeling of dependency and resentment.[9] Certain issues emerge from each strategy. While the issue of where the refugee shall fit into the class strata of the receiving society and how much social capital that society shall spend on language, cultural, and job training before refugees are expected to be self-sufficient has received different answers in other north Atlantic industrialized states,[10] most congregational sponsors (and many of the Volag representatives) have retained a historic model of ethnic stratification in the United States in their mind. New immigrants—whether they are European migrants of the nineteenth century or the Caribbean, Latin American, and Asian immigrants of the twentieth century—should start at the bottom of the ladder in menial, unskilled jobs and work their way up as did the European ethnics.

But unlike the European ethnics of the late nineteenth century, immigrants pushed and pulled by economic incentives, today's refugees are often people drawn from the middle and upper ranks of their society: this is especially likely to be the case in a communist state. The Vietnamese who came to the United States in 1975 after the fall of Saigon frequently had high statuses in South Vietnam and were well educated. They suffered both from the trauma of leaving their land forever without anticipation of any chance to return and from their subsequent downward mobility in the United States. To find an appropriate position in Riverside County for a former general, bank president, and head of the national art institute was impossible. By contrast, the Indochinese refugees of 1978 onward came from more heterogeneous backgrounds, had often already lost status, steady employment, and income since the unification of Vietnam and had fled in the face of crude coercion and extreme peril because they foresaw no future there. Furthermore, most were anxious and grateful to be admitted to the United States rather than to any other state. Most were initially quite willing to work. However, many saw schooling as a means to advance more rapidly in U.S. society than manual labor. New immigrants today are likely to be aware of the role education now plays in social mobility, a role more influential today than during the period of settlement of the European ethnics. The Southeast Asian refugees also knew of alternative ways to start out in the United States and differential benefits available in other states from their correspondence and conversation with other refugees. Such comparisons and the question of benefits and entitlements at times played a role in their readiness to accept the contract.

The First Phase

During the first phase of sponsorship, the sponsors, and especially the godparents, are observers and vicarious participants as well as helpers of the refugee households, absorbed by the interplay of culture, personality, and power. Gleaming through the ideal persona or social masks produced by Southeast Asian cultures emphasizing harmony, deference, and non-assertiveness in social relationships, are, one finds, young couples struggling with conflicts with in-laws, sons quarreling with fathers, boisterous children who have gone beyond their parents' control, and altercations between reunited branches of an extended family. Further, sponsors observe members of *their* family who are witty and dull, those who are eager to explore and those who do not take risks, those who are good natured and those who are withdrawn, and label and evaluate these as differences among all people. This also tends to reinforce the bond and individualize their attachment.

The commitment of godparents may result from the initial (presumably temporary) housing arrangements made by the committee. Hosts often became godparents and sometimes foster parents, as is the case of George and Kathy Gough. Their church sponsorship committee, headed by George, grew out of a prayer group that had been praying for the boatpeople. The night before their first organizational meeting, a mission priest in the United States called their denominational Volag in order to find sponsors for the families of two brothers whose children he had baptized in Southeast Asia. He was invited to speak at the organizational meeting at St. Christophers' (the Goughs' church), to which representatives of neighboring churches interested in sponsorship had also been invited. The latter were not ready to make a commitment, so the committee of St. Christopher voted to sponsor the two families, responding to the argument of one member that they had no right to separate a family that God had kept together. To their surprise, both families arrived the next week, a happening without parallel in my experience. The Goughs had agreed to house one family temporarily, expecting that the committee would rent a house or apartment within a week or two. To their greater surprise, the family the Goughs had volunteered to house on a temporary basis arrived without the mother (who had been detained with her infant child because of suspected tuberculosis) and stayed with them for three months. This was rather a shock, for Kathy said, from the beginning:

I had a lot of doubts and worries . . . I didn't want any part of it to tell you the truth Helen. George and these few people, they decided to take it on and I said, "Well, I'll help." . . . I guess I had a fear—it's human nature or something—of total commitment. At that time, I didn't understand how enormous an undertaking it is. I had seen everything on TV and read quite a bit but I tend to stand off and say, "Let somebody else do it." If I could help or contribute at some point, I'd do it. That's where George and I were until the day they arrived.

We had expected it to be like it was supposed to be—you get them an apartment. . . . It was somewhat of a surprise the way things turned out. . . . I had a lot of feelings and emotions the first 24 hours . . . sometimes your own family [which includes five children] is just too much and here to have four children whom you couldn't even speak with. I had a lot of sympathy for them and hoped I showed it . . . once you get that emotion out (I had a good cry), it readjusted . . . it was like being in a dark tunnel. You don't know when you're going to reach the end. That played a part in it because originally we thought it would be interim housing, at most a week . . . and then weeks passed and we ran into a lot of housing problems.

Homemaking was somewhat simplified by the church women bringing in dinner every night. But the usual chores that might be delegated to committees in a "regular" sponsorship were not, for, as Kathy said, "you don't call on a committee when someone under your own roof needs help." The bond was reinforced when Mai, the mother of the children Kathy had nurtured for two months, arrived.

I'll never forget meeting Mai. The first words she said were, "Kathy, next to God, nobody loves you as much as I do."

Reflecting upon other sponsorships, she concluded:

For me it was a more convincing way of partaking in this experience. . . . I've heard other sponsors like those at that meeting in Ionia [the county seat] speak in such an impersonal way: "Here they are and you do this and you do that." We really had an intimate relationship with these people and other sponsors were so cut and dried. You know what I mean? I sometimes got the feeling they were programmed to do the job they did and that's as far as they wanted to go. You know what I mean? I feel people should be friendly—should care for each other.

The most loving godparents, such as Kathy Gough, were not necessarily leaders nor people who were first committed to the sponsorship. Some, like Kathy, were drawn in because their spouse or friend was committed. Some expressed fear of foreigners. When the needs of particular refugees attracted them it evoked empathy, a compassion that sometimes became a passion, even when the need was thrust upon them involuntarily as it had been thrust on Kathy.

Playing host also created a special bond between Polly Miller, chair of St. Paul's Church Refugee Committee, and the Nuygens, Huang and Linh. Polly confesses it was love at first sight on her part. She hugged "the kids" (who were 24 and 20) at the first airport meeting "though I knew you weren't supposed to do it," she said, referring to her awareness of cultural differences in emotional expression in public and private situations. They had responded immediately. While they had been her houseguests for four weeks, it had been no burden but great fun. She did not ask them to do anything, knowing how household work might be interpreted by Indochinese refugees, but they had grabbed the vacuum cleaner and dustcloth after passing her a note saying, "We work." They had shared cooking and eating Chinese dishes (a favorite cuisine of the Millers) with them. Linh had called her "mama" and insisted that she be with her at the birth of her first child. This was a novel as well as an ecstatic experience for Polly, for she had had no children.

Such bonds as have been described may be hard for refugees and godparents to break once the refugees get their own apartment. When the bond is reciprocal, the relationship will continue. But living together is not always an uninterrupted love-fest, for differences between the refugee and sponsor's families over cooking, modes of bringing up children, and different conventional expectations of the houseguest role may cause tension. For example, most middle-class Americans expect that if they are houseguests they will share daily chores. Indochinese refugees may experience this demand as diminishing their status to that of servants and may comply without demurral in order to please their sponsors while suppressing their resentment. (Not all react this way, as the example of the Nuygens and the Millers show.) Refugee parents may experience a sudden loss of authority as their children relate directly to the sponsors, experiencing greater freedom with them and responding to rewards for just being and learning English—a skill in which they may soon surpass their parents.

Setting up refugees in a household of their own, obtaining medical care, getting jobs, and dealing with government bureaucracies always entail unexpected events and unanticipated problems. All leaders interviewed were asked what unexpected problems (and expected ones) occurred and how they were resolved, and these were classed by type (medical, familial, job-related, and so on) and seriousness in terms of how readily they could be resolved and whether they threatened the contract that united refugee and sponsor.

One aspect may appear surprising. The lack of communication was seldom perceived as a problem, although it was seen as a most important problem for the refugees by the few bilingual Vietnamese refugees of 1975 with whom I discussed refugee problems. Whereas some refugees arrived with a good command of written and spoken English, most had little or no ability to speak conversationally. But when there was good rapport, there was often a conviction among the sponsors that there was much greater cognition on their part than there was. One enthusiastic leader, Linda Valentine, replied when asked how they had communicated:

> I don't know. . . . It was lots of fun. . . . It's not hard to communicate as long as you have eyes.

Sponsors often relied on the bilingual Vietnamese refugees of 1975 as translators; at times the latter also served as cultural interpreters and friends of the newcomers, and at other times interpretation added a third level of cultural mediation, transforming words and affect conveyed by the sponsor and the refugee. Most of the 1975 refugees were glad to play this role at airport meetings, medical examinations, and other occasions when accurate understanding was indispensable. However, because most of those who were fluent in English were fully employed, attending school, or occupied full-time with young children, few had long stretches of free time, so on many occasions demanding two-way communication, sponsors and refugees had to devise ways to understand each other. The situation was more strained with the Lao refugees, for only one couple (both fully employed) were bilingual in Lao and English, so recent refugees with limited skills were often translating for sponsors of more recently arrived Lao refugees. At least one gynecological examination was conducted with the assistance of a telephone translator on a nationwide toll-free line for Indochinese refugees in Washington.

Nonverbal communication, picture books and Sears catalogs, and pocket bilingual dictionaries helped sponsors cope. But the sponsors' perception of mutual understanding is often a function of the shared warmth or feeling between sponsor and refugee rather than language, I discovered by an unintended test of second-hand reports of communications. My role (acting as a sponsorship developer) on occasion meant that I served as a broker to find new sponsors for relatives of refugees. Obtaining entry permits for a specific family necessitated that I get correct information on what was happening to them in a camp in Indonesia, so I had their letters to relatives in the United States translated by a bilingual Vietnamese college student on several occasions after having received summaries of the import of the letters from godparents who had spoken with the refugee to whom the letter was addressed. On all occasions, the summaries constructed by the godparents were incorrect in whole or in critical parts. They had constructed a coherent, dramatic, and appealing narrative from a few phrases or words that were often mistranslated. Rather than communication (that is, mutual cognition of a shared language) creating understanding, it appears that understanding leads to the perception of communication.

Understanding and accepting differences is important for the refugees to be accepted for who they are. As cultural guides, refugee sponsors could be classified on a continuum from assimilationists, who see their role as stripping away and replacing an old, useless, and scorned identity with a new one, to pluralists who respect the fact that the refugee is a mature person who had already incorporated coherent and appropriate cultural understandings, values, norms, and folkways and who try to teach the refugees what they need and want to know about the American language, practices, and values while helping them to maintain their own integrity. At the extreme, the assimilationist will strip the refugees of their given names—they will be renamed Nancy or Michael,—and their religion. This was not observed in our sample. The great majority of leaders interviewed appear to be cultural pluralists. A few encouraged church attendance, but church attendance itself was often self-reinforcing for refugees because of the warm response of congregants and the likelihood of being invited to dinner afterward. Most sponsors were pleased if the refugees attended their church regardless of their motives (usually termed "social" or "political") and accepting if they did not. If they had labeled themselves as Roman Catholic previous to arrival, non-Catholic sponsors informed them where they could attend Catholic services. In one instance, church sponsors arranged for a Buddhist priest to travel 75 miles to perform the mourning rites in commemoration of the anniversary of a death in the family of their refugees. Complaints of religious coercion or pressure voiced directly by refugees were rare in Riverside County.

Tensions and Problems in Sponsorship

Problems may arise among Indochinese refugees first from the trauma of flight, the loss of near relatives without times for grieving, and guilt over relatives left behind; these may be exacerbated (second) by family tensions predating those events or associated with them. Third, there are work, learning, and cultural readjustment problems inherent in all resettlement; and fourth, there are problems intrinsic to the relationship between sponsor and refugee. For the problems of flight, loss, and homelessness that lead to loneliness, grief, depression, and guilt feelings, there are no "solutions," but these may be eased by the support of other refugees and the presence of an ethnic community. Cultural estrangement may be gradually overcome by new bonds emerging and a growing sense of competence in English. Sponsors' sensitivity to such feelings, which may be expressed only indirectly through physical complaints, may help both sponsor and refugee.[11]

The other problems may be divided into those minor short-term ones that are readily resolvable by known techniques and longer-term problems that affect other areas of adjustment. More serious than these problems were problems of ends and immediate goals, which might jeopardize the contract and undermine the bond between refugees and sponsors. Most of the problems perceived by sponsors of these nineteen refugee households were of the former type; only one instance of the nineteen households could be called critical, and three called serious.

The most simple problems were medical. Children might arrive with skin rashes that needed treatment and contract intense toothaches that demanded immediate extraction. While cases of malaria and tuberculosis were reported infrequently (but regularly) among Indochinese refugees and intestinal parasites (which are not communicable) are common, the most common medical problem was dental caries. Child planning as well as childcare was considered an immediate need by many refugees. Several mothers asked for birth-control devices or requested surgical procedures. The demand for devices (which some were familiar with in Vietnam but had not been able to procure since 1975) provoked some hilarious and unexpected scenes when usually shy and undemanding women who could barely communicate in English appealed to female sponsors to demonstrate to their husbands the use of condoms. Ellen James recalled her embarrassment when she asked Roy, her minister, to run over to the Huynhs' apartment with a box of condoms. Roy found that Kay, another member of the committee, had already left a box and run out with explanation.

Some medical problems had longer-range implications. Persisting effects of trauma could be seen affecting a Cambodian refugee who experienced flashbacks that triggered cold sweats. Some sympathetic but psychiatrically unaware committee members saw this as a symptom of personal disability and proposed treating it as such, but others on the committee persuaded them that this was a normal response to an abnormal situation.

In other instances, war injuries had long-term effects. One man needed reparative surgeries, which turned out to be several minor operations, which meant the postponement (and eventual loss) of a promised job. In another case, the refugee had a collapsed lung and endured unexpressed suffering from standing all day in a machine shop. (He eventually quit for several reasons.) Sponsors reacted sympathetically to these problems and sought the most effective treatment whenever treatment was possible. (Medicaid usually took care of hospital costs.) More difficult to cope with were the fears an unlabeled sickness and foreign medical procedures instigated. A thirty-five-year-old woman who had almost fainted in her English class was taken to the hospital and tested for diagnosis. She became terrified, believing they were draining her blood and she would die.

Tensions or issues within the refugee household arose as often as medical problems and often were not simple to resolve. In some cases the household units that had formed in flight or in the camps proved brittle. Fictive kinship relations seem to have been constructed in camps by friends isolated from their nuclear families in order that they might go to the United States together. A third person of the same age who was nominally a cousin of the young couple with whom he or she lived might soon leave the area if he or she found another relative elsewhere in the

United States. But splitting up was not always a realistic solution for fictive or real kin. A brother and sister (both in their twenties) living together who seemed to have reached a personal impasse expected the sponsor to resolve their problem by setting up each of them in separate apartments. The sponsors, joined by members of the Vietnamese community, counseled them that they would have to learn to resolve their own problems and live together until or unless they were financially able to live separately.

Sponsors often turned to the Vietnamese priest Father Paul for counseling, as did refugees. But some problems that signaled changes in the structure and functioning of families were not reversible but required new adaptations. One refugee couple seemed to have lost control of their children in the refugee camps and found they had become more aggressive and boisterous than the parents were accustomed to, characteristics that would probably be reinforced in the schools of Riverside County. The godparents felt it necessary to directly advise the refugees and exert their authority over the children despite the general injunction not to interfere in parent-child relations. In another case, the temporary separation of an extended family by the sponsor (pressed by the limits on tenants imposed by the landlord of the donated housing) led to two permanent households, the loss of authority by the father, and the assimilation of one of the younger children into the household of the aunt. The change in power relations could also be attributed to the fluent English spoken by the aunt, who soon became the intermediary and spokesperson for the family, and the rapid Americanization of the children who had lived with a member of the committee (who became their godparent). Regardless of how sponsors viewed the unanticipated consequences of their impact on the refugees, the basic configuration of the family could not be restored by regret or nostalgia once it had changed. (In the latter case, the leader of the sponsoring committee regretted the part played by the committee and advised new sponsors against separation of families for any reason.) But such changes within immigrant families (if not the pace of change) have been repeated over one hundred years, and it seems unlikely that the generational conflicts induced by differences in assimilation and different cultural reference groups could be avoided by the Indochinese refugees. This (and another refugee family) would be subjected to more American influences and their roots extended when two fluent English-speaking young women (one Vietnamese and one Lao) married young American men whom they had met at the time their fiancées served in the armed forces and the diplomatic service in Indochina.

The bond between sponsor and refugee was not tested or frayed by such problems; indeed, they might create further empathy. Only an unresolved disagreement about the contract—the mutual expectations and obligations of refugee and sponsor—might test that bond. This occurred in two of the thirteen sponsoring committees surveyed and affected three of the nineteen refugee households sponsored. The conflict was successfully resolved in one instance involving one committee and two refugee households, and in the other case, the sponsorship was cut short by the departure of the refugees who had resided in Riverside County less than two months.

The first was a family reunification case involving the sponsorship of two families related to a Vietnamese refugee who had come to Riverside County in 1975. The perceived misunderstandings between the refugees and the sponsoring committee of the Church of Christ the Carpenter was exacerbated by continuous tension between the relative and the committee leaders. The latter perceived the relative's attention as continuous and inconsistent intervention or meddling without cooperation. In turn, the relative perceived the leader(s) as inconsistent, unreliable, and autocratic. During the controversy, each saw the other as the sole source of the problem. The committee chairs were displeased about the lack of progress of the refugees in learning English (which the latter would not use with them) and in getting or retaining a job. The men lost their first job because of lack of understanding directions, and the sponsors feared that they were not eager to find another one and wanted to go on welfare. Repeated counseling of *all* parties clarified the controversy, causing the sponsors to modify some misperceptions, change their plans, and convey their expectations for a time frame in which they expected the refugees to become self-supporting to them in a nonthreatening manner. They did so and both men obtained jobs with local employers that seemed to satisfy the sponsors and the refugees' relative and that they still held at the time of my interview (six months later).

The difficulties were exacerbated in this case by the lack of a strong, direct, affective bond between the sponsors and the refugees. Although the former showed much sympathy for the latter, reserving the brunt of criticism for the relative, there was little feeling, few friendly exchanges, and no laughter in the relations between sponsor and refugee in contrast to most such relationships. No member of the committee visited socially with either refugee household to have a cup of tea, play cards, or enjoy other kinds of nonverbal sociability. The sense of social distance between refugees and sponsors was explicit. The difficulties of the refugees were ascribed to their rural background, their intimidation in Vietnamese re-education and refugee camps, which rendered them speechless at the initial meeting, afraid to test out their English "because they were afraid of being beaten if they made a mistake." "They'd never make it in Saigon," a Vietnamese war bride who arrived in the United States in 1973 was reported to have commented.

The most critical case in which the bond was tested involved a joint sponsorship of two churches. The committee sponsored a young couple (the Rucs) with the wife's two brothers. The husband, Anh, spoke excellent English. Both husband and wife had advanced professional and technical training in Vietnam, training that could not be put to use here for years without reaccreditation, examination, and certification. Issues dividing the Rucs and the committee focused on autonomy, entitlement, and their perception of relative deprivation: what status were they to start at and who should decide what they would get and when.

Signs of trouble appeared before the Rucs' arrival. Division of opinion within the committee formed about the part played by the Masons who turned out to be the Rucs' patron and godparents. The Masons furnished the apartment rented by the committee with tasteful antiques they had discarded, and matched linens and shower curtains. Other members of the committee compared it with the apartments of their children at college or their own first homes, sensing theirs was the inferior, leading to more envy of the Masons who, some felt, "had gone overboard." Entitlement seems to have been the unspoken issue: were new refugees in the United States entitled to start out at this level?

When the Rucs arrived, Elizabeth Mason had not finished putting up the pictures. Anh wanted to put them on the wall himself and picked up a hanger. "No, no, Anh, you can't do it!" Elizabeth said.

Anh kept testing what he could do, decide and get for and by himself. Lorraine Ferante, the chair, recalls that:

> What blew everybody's cool was that Anh wanted to buy a color TV with the $480 from the agency. I could understand how Bill Brown (the treasurer) just about had a heart attack. . . .

He had the set all picked out in a store in an adjacent shopping center and knew the Volag grant (which check he had to endorse) was made out to him and the United Churches Committee. Because the sponsors believed this to be a misuse of the money, which was intended for basic support and a minimal nest egg for the refugee, and they expected to draw upon it for the support of the Rucs when their resources ran out, they refused.

More basic were the differences between Anh's plans and those of the committee for his future. Anh's evaluation of education may have been raised by the affluent Masons, who first played host to the refugees at a dinner after their arrival in their architect-designed wall-to-wall carpeted home. Lorraine Ferante describes that night:

> We were there that night but I could not believe what went on. . . . Anh said: "This is like the President's house in Vietnam." . . . Elizabeth had said, "I want to show you the house, Anh. This is just a typical American house." Later,

Walter Mason said, "If you study real hard, Anh, you can live like this too." I nearly fell over—his own place or ours must look like chicken coops if this was a typical American house.

Anh wanted to go to a local community college and get public assistance for support. The committee had an offer for him for a $200 a week job at IAW (significantly higher than the wage and status of jobs obtained by most refugees) and offered him private tutoring. He turned both down.

The issue of funding an education at the local community college (assuming that it would further Anh's long-range plan) might have been resolved without compromising the committee's objections to public assistance had there not been basic mistrust between Anh, the committee chair, and core members. Other refugees had obtained scholarships and work-study jobs at the local community college; furthermore, there were three other members of the family would could (and were) working full time so they might have taken turns studying and working. What caused this mistrust and the fraying of the bond between them was the perception of the leaders and many core committee members that Anh saw them only as instrumentalities, turning the bond to an exchange relationship. They agreed he was a manipulator, consciously using one member against the other to get as much as possible for himself. As Lorraine Ferante put it:

I really couldn't believe it. . . . He didn't reciprocate. . . . We were holding out our hand.

Anh's consciousness of sexual and social hierarchy and his determination to be on top was made explicit to them as a result of his excellent command of English. (This again is disproof of the truism that communication brings people closer; in this instance it clarified the cause of the division between them.) Anh told the women on the committee guiding him that they did not know what they were doing and challenged the competence of Lorraine. He was eager to determine the ranking of races and ethnic groups in the United States, Lorraine recalled:

He was very concerned as to who was on the lowest rung of the ladder. I said, "Well, Anh, I think right now it's the Mexican-Americans." That seemed to relieve him.

The committee was divided over the interpretation of Anh's expectations. His affluent godparents, the Masons, believed he was being misinterpreted. Others believed that the Masons were at fault for raising his aspirations unduly by giving expensive gifts, holding up their life-style as a model, and "not leveling with him." Both Anh and some committee members seem to have been experiencing a competitive sense of relative deprivation. Anh's claims to entitlement to a subsidized education instigated comparison among the members of the committee with the deprivations of their children and the debts they incurred for higher education. Here Anh was asking for wall-to-wall carpeting and a color TV for the apartment and refusing to combine paid employment and study. Their expectation that the Rucs would accept their changed status was rapidly shaken. Lorraine reflected that:

> I thought we were helping someone who was really deprived . . . (but) they had a good education in Vietnam. They did want their freedom which I can understand but they also wanted everything . . . they wanted everything right off the bat.

Anh too may have felt relatively deprived and frustrated as he compared his present position to his former status in Vietnam and realized he was hemmed in by his dependence on sponsors, patrons who, he felt, were keeping him from exploiting opportunities (such as free schooling) that he had heard that refugees were entitled to elsewhere. His lack of autonomy was signified to him by the sponsors' unwillingness to let him have the Volag check.

The Rucs went to California, the favorite state of Vietnamese refugees for relocation, within two months. Lorraine Ferante confessed she felt intense relief, while others voiced some resentment that they had left so soon. The Rucs wrote and called, broadly hinting they'd like their furniture sent on (at the committee's expense). The committee ignored their request and gave the furniture to another sponsorship committee expecting a refugee family soon. The Rucs wrote again requesting the disputed check from the Volag. After some turmoil, debate, and consultation with the Volag, they sent the check.

In the two committees experiencing the conflict described, the bond between sponsors and refugees was tested, and in one found wanting. Both the characteristics and attitudes of the refugees themselves evoked different judgments and feelings. In the first case of The Church of Christ the Carpenter, the committee leaders looked down on the refugees but showed sympathy for them. The leaders of the United Churches Committee appeared to perceive the Rucs as social equals, but had mixed feelings toward Anh, both of admiration and resentment. Other members of the family emerged as shadowy characters. Lorraine Ferante recalled that:

> He was really a charmer, very amusing to have around, enchanting with the children. It was great until you got down to the nitty-gritty.

And Mary Lou Smith, the first cochair of the committee, said:

> I give them a lot of credit. . . . Anh's very ambitious for them. They'll go places. . . . Of course it was frustrating to me because he expected so much so soon. He only wanted the best for them.

The situation of the two committees, seemingly so different, is similar in that both the sponsorships became a three-party situation or triad with the refugees confronted with two competing models or authorities. In the case of the Church of Christ the Carpenter, the competing models were the committee leaders on the one hand and the refugee's relative on the other; the relative, a relatively successful refugee, was apprehended by the committee leaders to have a secret agenda in competition with theirs. The United Churches Committee was split between the Masons (at times leading a faction and at times single patrons) and the core leaders of the committee. As in these cases, triads usually turn into coalitions of two against one. [12]

The fact that the key leaders of both committees felt they had become the minority of one, unable to control the situation much of the time, demands explanation. One factor that may have exacerbated the problems that emerged was the malfunctioning of both committees: in one case this was caused by lack of cohesion and in the other lack of group involvement in determining goals and priorities. The lack of cohesion and acrimony within the United Churches Committee and the feeling of isolation of the leader was not reported in other joint sponsorships or interfaith committees embracing many congregations. In this case, it seems to be singularly related to the lack of previous bonds between the churches, the schism within one church, the failure of clergy to serve a unifying role, and the early breakdown of joint leadership due to health problems of one leader. While there was no reported acrimony in the Church of Christ the Carpenter Committee, there was hardly any committee functioning for virtually all decisions were made by one or both coleaders so that the support and self-examination that emerges from the group and that might have led to a more creative approach to their problems and short-cut the cycle of misperceptions was lacking.

The Functioning of Refugee Committees

Looking backward, it seems amazing how well most of these committees worked. Unlike most voluntary associations, the urgency of the tasks and the unpredictability of needs demanded that leaders press, cajole, and otherwise induce lagging officers and members to perform or resign. The committee became a family united in kinship to *their* family, but a family starting out as adults with about equal status, age, and claims to authority. Members could be seen creating new roles (such as godparents), usurping roles, and improvising new solutions to problems. Social control had to be exercised at times within committees to prevent the behavior of members from jeopardizing the sponsorship, to avoid factions or patronage relations developing with the refugees, and to prevent polarization or misunderstanding between the church and the committee.

How sponsorship committees work cannot be understood simply by examing the formal structure or division of labor based on functions. (To be sure, the sense of equity in mutual guarantee of participation this provides was a good baseline.) Group discussion bringing up different interpretations and views of the same situation served to enlarge each member's perspectives on individual and cultural differences, enabled people to perceive different ways in which the same situation might be construed, and often put what might be classed as a problem into perspective. For example, in one committee, Liz will report with irritation how Thanh greeted them on the lawn yesterday in his undershorts. Howard asks rhetorically how should people who see their neighbors ambling around outdoors in swim trunks and tennis briefs realize that it is not the level of dress or undress here that determines propriety but the labeling of garments as indoor or outdoor wear.

More possible solutions, skills, and resources usually exist within the group than in any single individual. In a trusting sponsorship committee, members can voice their differences (and sometimes their perceptions of others working at cross purposes) and ventilate potential sources of hostility. General tensions are discharged, morale renewed, and people revived and united by laughter at absurdities that are not for public sharing.

In one committee, Mike tells of a new incident:

> You know that eccentric Mrs. Jones up the road called me last week to tell me her cat had been missing for a week. "What does that have to do with us?" I asked. "The Vietnamese eat cats, you know," she said. She insisted that the Nuygens had spirited it away and consumed it. I told her that I was sure that wasn't so but I'd ask Van just to assure her for her peace of mind. So I went over and said, "Van, I'm going to ask you an embarrassing question. It's embarrassing for me to ask it." "What does embarrassing mean?" he asked. "You'll know after I ask you," I replied.

And in another, Jack tells his story:

> So, Loc and I were windowshopping in the Woodview Plaza and we passed this pet shop with a poodle for $325 in the window. "They make a very nice dish," he said seriously. I nearly broke up laughing.

Most committees were structured similarly (as has been described) and appeared to work well, with their members reportedly enjoying each other. A committee with minimal structure (in a congregation with as minimal a structure) did not work as well, its leader reported, because of the lack of coordination of action and information, the unresponsiveness of members to emergent needs of the refugees, and the omission and duplication of roles.

Unintended (or unexpected) consequences occasionally arose from the sexual division of labor in committees. The self-selection of women for most of the home-centered roles seemed to be inevitable, for these women on these committees had much more time than the men during the day when appointments at school, clinic, doctors, and governmental social-service offices had to be made. But this meant that refugees who were accustomed to a patriarchal social structure might see their lives as being dominated by women in authoritative roles daily. In a few cases (usually involving young Indochinese men), tension was evident, as in the case of the United Church Committee.

Most leaders reported a decline of commitment as time went on among peripheral members of the committee, and other church members asked to perform occasional chores such as driving. Volunteers no longer came forth; they had to be recruited. Often leaders would perform such chores themselves regardless of whether it was in an area they had initially volunteered for. Instigating people to fulfill commitments and coordinating action was a persisting chore (if not a problem) in all sponsorships.

The question of commitment again illustrates how the extraordinary demands of refugee sponsorship do not fit into the conventional institutionalized patterns of voluntary action. Commitment cannot be fitted into a regular time slot every week; needs change and emerge at unpredictable times often. But each volunteer has his/her own time-budget. In practice, the one-time or short-term commitment of the many is compensated for by the increased commitment of the few who have developed a stronger bond with the refugees themselves. Since no one knows to begin with who will become godparents and develop a more intense bond, if more people are initially drawn in, there is more likelihood this will emerge spontaneously.

While leaders often become godparents, godparents also emerge in totally unforeseen ways. In one case, the rental agent of the apartment complex in which the committee rented an apartment became a big brother to the eldest son of the refugee family and a godparent of the whole family, although he was initially adverse to renting to them because of their number and previous unfortunate experiences he had had with foreigners. He was coopted in the committee the week after he agreed to request the management to rent to them.

Succeeding Phases: Independence and Departures

Moving from the provider phase and achieving autonomy of the refugee household was a goal of all sponsors but a goal pursued in different ways. How soon this was accomplished can be related to the size of the refugee household, the goals and strategies pursued, and the resources of sponsors.

Refugee households ranged from two to seven persons: two-thirds were made up of four or fewer persons. The ratio of household members who might be employed to the total refugee household range from 1:7 to 7:7. It was a young population: a 1980 survey of new Indochinese refugees in Riverside County showed that only 7 percent were over thirty-five years old. In two-thirds of the households, half or more of their members could work full-time. Smaller households, which had a higher ratio of members in the labor force, had a better chance of making an adequate living sooner.

At the time the interviews were conducted (which was from six to twenty-four months after the refugees had arrived), twelve of the nineteen households had become wholly or predominantly self-supporting. Five other families had left the area before becoming self-sufficient although one or more wage-earners had been working in four of them. Among the households resident in the area that had become self-supporting, one head of household was later assisted by the family's sponsor to return to school for a Survival English course as a preliminary to enrollment in an apprentice program because he was unable to earn an adequate living on which to support a family of eight at his previous unskilled occupation and found his health endangered by workplace conditions there. Also, five among them were receiving some financial assistance from their sponsors (who might pay for auto or medical insurance) although they worked full or part-time, and two were living in low-cost church housing. Several of them were attending a local community college and working.

In seven of the twelve households that had become self-supporting and were still resident in Riverside County, the principal wage-earners had obtained jobs and become independent within three months of their arrival; the others took from five to eight months. In three of these cases, this was a function of the sponsor's strategy. In two others (previously discussed), this was caused by the refugees' inability to get or retain jobs. The two households that were most dependent on sponsors had arrived within the preceding six months; jobs were found for their members soon after their sponsors sought employment. For one of these households, supplementary public assistance was drawn upon by sponsors for a sixteen-year-old student who was not considered by the adult household members part of their kin group or their dependent.

The two instances of refugees who had not been able to retain jobs were of refugees with virtually no English or living skills on arrival. Sponsors followed no common (or evident) single rule regarding when they expected refugees to become independent; several committes paid for housing for months after the refugee household's members in the work force were fully employed.

Most refugees got minimum-wage jobs in unskilled factory work or service occupations—cleaner, dishwasher, motel maid, nurse's aide, bus-boy—but a few obtained semiskilled jobs—a seamstress and an auto-mobile and motorcycle repair mechanic. Virtually all jobs—advertised or unadvertised—were secured by the sponsor locating the job or accom-panying the refugee to the interview; many were elicited by and from church members who were employers.

The majority of sponsors heeded the advice of Father Paul and tried to give refugees an intensive period in which to study Survival English in a county-wide vocational training program funded by the Department of Labor without pressing them to work. The utility of this prescription, given this facility, became questionable, and some refugees preferred to drop out of it and work sooner than their sponsors planned.[13]

For the refugees to achieve autonomy meant not only becoming self-supporting but also to be able to function without daily continuing ser-vices such as contributed transportation, and to be able to help to resolve their own problems and to make their own decisions. A few leaders were aware and troubled that their role involved taking over the refugees' lives, making decisions, and doing things for them they might have done for themselves. Frank Myerhof told of a division within his committee on this point:

> Some felt they ought to be allowed to make their own decisions but others thought that they didn't have the input. . . . We did too much for them. . . . I'm not sure that it was right supporting them for so long but the committee was willing. . . . We were impressed by Father Paul's advice.

Linda Valentine and Ellen James also said (separately), "We did too much for them." Doing too much often meant they did things for them—obtained a job or an apartment—rather than showing them how to do it because it was so much easier. It might mean reinforcing the refugees' dependency by getting a job necessitating constant rides (given the un-availability and limited schedules of public transportation) rather than a job nearby. It might mean continuing to contribute services, such as car repairs, for which the sponsors, as consumers, would ordinarily pay. Another form of doing too much was that of patrons (as observed earlier) and godparents giving too many and too expensive gifts. This may create a double bind for the refugees: while grateful, they are demeaned as their role as a client is reinforced, for they cannot reciprocate. When the gifts are given to the children, the parents may feel their authority is further diminished, for their role as a provider has been further undermined.

Usually the refugees avidly sought to achieve autonomy, sometimes despite the sponsors' unintended reinforcement of their dependency. In-frequently, refugees were perceived to be manipulating the sponsor as a provider and patron as has been described.

One sponsorship was unique in that the sponsors had talked to many previous sponsors prior to the arrival of their refugees and had decided that previous sponsors were guilty of "smothering" the refugees with their attention and oversolicitude. They decided to set them up as a household, get them jobs, and wait for them to call if they needed help. Arthur Brown tells how:

> . . . we always called before we went over. . . . We wanted to respect their privacy. We had the open house for them at their apartment rather than at the church because they wanted it there.

The affective bond appeared as close in this sponsorship as any, but more equality and space for separation was allowed. Arthur relates how:

> . . . at first they were very respectful . . . later we were all kissing and hugging.

Perhaps the most frustrating experience for the sponsor is the departure of the refugees before both parties have recognized their autonomy. Seven of nineteen households, or 37 percent of those sponsored by the committees in the sample, had left before the time of the interviews, usually for California. This, in itself, is not surprising given the experience in Riverside County in 1975 and the knowledge of secondary migration of Indochinese refugees outside the major states of concentration. In most cases, a desire or obligation to reunite with other relatives here was given as the motive. News and rumors from other refugees of higher wage rates, generous welfare benefits, and free schooling available in California (any training program housed in a community college may be labeled as college) and an offer of temporary housing by a friend were all incentives to leave along with the balmy weather, although the latter was more openly talked about than materialistic inducements. Most of the refugee households who had been in Riverside County for more than six months and were still there at the time of the interviews had relatives in Riverside County before they came or had persuaded their sponsors to also sponsor their relatives, which seems to indicate that the desire to be near family is a motive for staying as well as leaving. However, preliminary data from a major northeast metropolitan area do not confirm the expectation (were this hypothesis correct) that refugees with relatives in the area were more likely to stay.[14] At the time of the interviews, there were three extended families of Vietnamese and Laotian refugees in Riverside County, each composed of two to four nuclear families. Although there were a few instances of refugees with relatives in Riverside County leaving (often to join other relatives), proportionately more refugees without family there left.

Sponsors' attitudes toward refugees' departures during this second phase (before autonomy is recognized) recalled in recollection ranged from mixed acceptance—"Of course, we missed them just as you would miss a good friend but it was the best thing for them"—to categorical rejection. Recounting their response, feelings from regretful acceptance to intense disappointment were expressed. Where the relationship between the refugees and the sponsors involved overt conflict (as in the case of the United Churches Committee), resentment was also expressed. Commonly, after the initial surprise, one or more members of the committee closest to the refugees would interrogate them to explore how firm was their intent, how realistic was their perception of what they could expect at their destination, and whether they understood the implications of being on their own. They would appraise whether specific arrangements had been made for housing and travel, such arrangements confirming to them the intentions and capability of the refugees. After this was confirmed, they returned to their part as a mentor or counselor, discussing with the refugees how to give notice (in some cases they insisted on two weeks notice being given) and get references from their employers, advising how to cut off household utilities and get deposits back, how to transfer school and medical records, and consummate travel arrangements—sometimes they drove them to the airport. Frequently, they gave a party for the departing family. Sometimes a sponsor gave financial aid to cover travel costs. However, in all these cases, the plan to leave was based on using the savings of the refugee or money sent by relatives for travel.

Most active members of the committee accepted (or pretended to accept) the departure with equanimity for which they had been prepared—to anticipate such a move by other sponsors (and by the RIC Sponsorship Development Project)—and to view it as a sign of growth, confidence, and expression of freedom. But a few leaders who were more involved did not. These voiced their apprehension that the refugees were leaving prematurely, could not take care of themselves without their aid, and/or would fall into a marginal existence in an ethnic ghetto, far inferior to the life-style they deserved and could have made for themselves had they stayed in their town. Ellen James recalls her feelings on this score six months later:

> I was very upset about it myself. . . . I didn't want to keep them here . . . but I just felt they were going into a stiuation which wasn't as good as the one here where they were well established but you have to put that against family, how much their family meant to them and their tradition and culture. . . . Loi really felt bad because we had given him so much and he felt he was betraying us. . . . I didn't really feel that but I told him if he got out there and ever wanted to come back to let us know.

Several tentative explanations might be advanced for the intensity of departure responses during this period before recognition of the refugee's autonomy. Departure may be seen as a threat or mark the loss and invalidation of the sponsor's role without their concurrence. If the sponsor sees her or himself as a tutor, the refugee must be tutored. If the sponsors see themselves as parents, the refugee leaving is a rejecting or defiant child. The resocialized refugee in either case is the product of the sponsor.

But the sense of loss may also be viewed as an unanticipated consequence of the intensity of the bond between sponsor and refugee and the lack of consummation of the relationship in equality and reciprocity. This sponsor does not unconsciously seek the refugee's dependence but their independence. This was best expressed by Linda Valentine. To Linda, sponsorship itself was a sacrament, an expression of her deepest religious values. She had been moved to tears by the sight of men, women, and, especially, children dying at sea. Her total immersion in the sponsorship as coordinator, godparent, and friend had been amply repaid, she felt. When asked how she felt about all the time it took, adding to her daily schedule constructed around the needs of three young children, she said:

I didn't resent it. At the beginning, I used to come home singing and joyous, thankful to the Lord that I'd had the opportunity to hold one of those babies that were on the boat. We felt like this was a personal blessing. We were not helping them. *They* were helping *us*. Of course when you're in the middle of these things, you get angry at the food stamp people at social services [who kept on making mistakes], at the landlady, etc. No one resented it.

This was not only an act of communion, but the relationship was a source of reward.

They just became good friends. And the kids were so fantastic together. And you know how you'll always help a friend out.

She enjoyed going places with them, exchanging recipes and sharing dinners, and was exhilarated by people's reactions when they went out together, Loi holding her fair-haired two year old, Billy, and she hugging their dark-haired baby, Li. She looked forward not to keeping them as wards or clients but to change them into peers and retain them as friends:

It was awful that they were leaving because they'd become such good friends of ours . . . and it was that day I'd got that house [to move them from the first house in which the landlady gave them so much trouble] so I felt this double disappointment. . . . It was very tense. . . .

I was frustrated that they left. . . . I cried and cried—not that I resented their leaving but there was so much work put in it. I just fantasized about the day we could all sit down together and Mai and Loi could talk and they could finally tell us what it was like for them: these would be the memories we could discuss some day and we've been denied that. *It's like having a stillborn child. You've gone through all the months of pregnancy and labor and it's wasted.* That's how I felt. We were just starting to reap some of the rewards; we went through all the pains and they were becoming American—not that I'm a flagwaver or that patriotism is the thing—and independent.

After their departure, the predominant feeling would be fatigue on her part and several others. Once the exhilaration was over, the letdown set in. Active committee members all said, "Don't call me," and they had not yet had a meeting to consider another sponsorship (although ample funds remained) nor disposed of the treasury five months after the refugees had left.

Linda's response to an aborted relationship may be compared to that of the Goughs, who also saw their experience as a sacrament and experienced as or more intense a bond than Linda. For had they not lived together for three months, nurturing the children before their mother arrived, until they finally saw themselves as an extended family so that when the Ngos left (something so eagerly anticipated at the beginning), being alone seemed like a wrenching separation? After the Ngos had a home of their own, they were frequent visitors to the Gough home. Van looked to George for tutoring, Kathy and Mai chatted, and the children were fast friends. While the timing and constancy of having friends one sees so often might wear on some, the Goughs would no more think of withholding themselves than they would have cut short a telephone conversation with a favorite aunt—although they might have their own concerns they'd rather get back to than listen. Their closeness as families was reinforced by their attendance at the same church and that of their children at the same parochial school. (This coincidence resulted from the fact that the Goughs' church had been recruited as sponsors by the mission priest who had baptized a child in this family in the Asian refugee camp.) At the time of the interview, eighteen months after the arrival of the Ngos, the Goughs viewed them just as good friends, but they seem like the kind of friends who have become extended family. "They're the best friends I've ever had," says Kathy. The pictures of the Ngos' children are on their mantelpiece together with those of their own children and several of all the children together. The Goughs shared Christmas dinner with them, and when their relatives visit, they ask about the Ngos as a matter of course.

How refugees and sponsors enact the next phase—becoming "just friends"—depends on the physical distance and the earlier bonds they've established and the degree of separation with which both feel most comfortable. By contrast, Arthur Brown had a very different relationship with Huynh Hung, whom he had never lived with and who had become autonomous in four months. Arthur's church (as has been described) had decided to respect their privacy. The Huynhs, who came here with a fair command of English, made clear their desire to drop out of the full-time ESL program in which their sponsors had enrolled them because they felt it was not helping them and they wanted to go to work. The sponsors left the decision up to them; some preferred to have them go to school longer. At the time of the interview, Arthur Brown remarked that their family had not seen the Huynhs for some time because the latter were so busy with full-time jobs and pursuing advanced English courses at night. Arthur was also working nights because of the seasonal demands of his job. He talked about inviting the Huynhs to dinner, but it seemed apparent that he was confident that their relationship would continue on a casual, friendly basis regardless of whether they dined together next week, next month, or in a few months.

One example of a continuing casual but caring friendship with Vietnamese refugees sponsored in 1975 is that of Bruce Gerzuny and the Locs. Bruce was among the six leaders interviewed belonging to four congregations that had sponsored Vietnamese refugees in 1975 and was among the four out of six who considered the experience positive. The family sponsored by his congregation is the only one of the families sponsored by these four congregations still in Riverside County. Bruce seldom sees the Locs but they talk on the phone from time to time.

> He's still here . . . he called us tonight by phone . . . we're friends. . . . He calls me from time to time to ask for help or talk. I helped him recently to negotiate a deal to buy a new car. He knew just what he wanted—I had recommended the brand my wife drives—but he knew he could get a better deal with me than alone.

The Locs, who live in the same housing project as do the new refugees whom Bruce's church is sponsoring, are helping the latter although they come from a different nation and only can speak English together.

Bruce takes great pride in the success of the Locs:

> The people we've brought here will be good citizens, good for this country. The Locs have sent five children to college on full scholarship of whom two have already graduated magna cum laude. . . . When he walked in to church with them on New Year's Eve straight and tall in their best clothes I just beamed.

Sponsors of Indochinese refugees in 1979–80 who are self-supporting and still in Riverside County report seeing them fairly often as friends. Although their friendship has many instrumental functions for the refugees (which the sponsors acknowledge), they are apt to stress the refugees' genuine concern for them and the rewards they got out of the experience. Focusing on the refugees who have moved, I asked the leaders of these committees when they had last heard from them, how they communicated, who initiated the communication, how often they heard from them, and explored their feeling of whether they were still in touch or if communication had lapsed. At the time of these interviews, the seven refugee households that had moved had been gone from one to sixteen months; four had left within six to eight months. Holiday greetings and telephone calls were common. Leaders of one committee feared communications had lapsed and expressed nostalgia and disappointment, but subsequently communication was resumed.

The United Churches Committee leaders who had experienced such conflict in their relationship did not expect to hear from the Rucs again after they sent them the Volag check, which the latter had requested, and expressed no desire to hear from them further.

Assessments of Sponsorships

Despite its great diffusion as a means of resettlement in the United States, no study has evaluated congregational or group sponsorship and other types of sponsorship—individual, institutional, and relatives. Nor does this study make such a claim, but one can begin to identify what preliminary kinds of questions one should ask and data one can look at.

The manifest function of the sponsoring committee was fulfilled by all but one of the fourteen committees. The others brought nineteen households composed of eighty-one refugees to Riverside County. In no case did a sponsor default on their obligation to support and be responsible for the primary needs of the refugees before the latter became autonomous. In eighteen of these nineteen sponsorships (95 percent), sponsors and refugees continued to work together for mutual goals despite problems or (in two cases) issues and perceptions that threatened conflicts. Refugees were reported to have become more autonomous and better able to communicate in English in these eighteen cases. In the nineteenth case, there was little evidence of improvement in two of three family members, and basic mistrust and disagreement on strategy and goals divided the sponsors and refugees.

This seems to me to be substantive prima facie evidence that congregational sponsorship served its intended social function well. One may also ask what were the costs and the rewards involved.[15]

The unanticipated consequences of sponsorship, almost all leaders felt, were the rewards and fulfillment they enjoyed that more than compensated for the costs. None denied the costs. It had been psychically exhilarating at times and wearing at other times but always costly in terms of their own time agendas. Most had no idea of how much time they had contributed, but two-thirds estimated it took over ten hours a week in the beginning (the first month of resettlement) and almost half of these estimated it took over twenty hours. Most of the leaders who estimated spending less than ten hours weekly were the first mobilizers who initiated the commitment and then passed the leadership on to a committee chair or a more active cochair. While most of those initially putting in between ten and twenty hours a week during the first month after the refugees' arrival reported some decline after that, the majority of those putting in over twenty hours a week did not. The latter, all of whom were women who were not in the labor force, appear to have become wholly absorbed by the sponsorship as by a vocation. Virtually all accepted this with goodwill, scarcely any reporting annoyance or resentment of the refugees' needs. Resentment was evoked by problems resulting from demoralization, rivalry, or lack of organization within two of the fourteen committees.

When asked how they felt now about the whole experience, virtually all are positive although some remark on some change they ought to have made or reflect on their mistakes. They express pride in the outcome, delight in their accomplishment, and enjoyment of the unexpected consequences—how much they have been the beneficiaries in the relationship. The latter sense is greater when the refugee family is still there and diminished when the sponsor views the departure as aborting the relationship. Doing the Lord's work is most important to some such as Arthur Brown, who is

. . . reluctant to take credit . . . that would involve pride. But it's not my doing but the Lord's doing . . . just something that had to be done.

If anything it was all rewarding. . . . You try to tell people the benefits you've received and they can't comprehend it.

Kathy Gough, who recalled that at the beginning, "I didn't want any part of it," and credited the original leadership to her husband, stressed how much she had grown and how much more capable she felt, concluding:

It's the greatest experience of my life. . . . I relate to people on a more spiritual level now . . . before, all I used to care for was me, Kathy.

Frank Myerhof, who at first did not volunteer for any committee and doubted that his church could bring it off (he was dubious about the usefulness of prayer at organizing meetings) and later became chair when asked by the first mobilizer (head of the prayer group), said sponsorship is "one of the most exciting things I've ever done." In both Frank's and Cathy's case, altruism—regardless of the original motivation—had become a means for self-expression and confirming one's identity, as Ralph Turner noted it might be.[16]

The most common assessment was that of Irene Carlson: "We got more out of it than they did." Any sign of reciprocity shown by the refugees—sharing dishes, inviting sponsors to birthday parties (a custom picked up from them), giving their children grapes and cookies, inviting them to tea—signifies to them that the bond is mutual. Sofia and David Armond told me that the Bao family was so concerned about them, they hesitated to tell them when they were sick or had a mishap. When their teenage son, Roger, had been in an auto accident from which he emerged unscathed, Bao Ling, matriarch of the family, marched in and without speaking tied white strings around his wrist to restore his errant well-being. The use of such amulets is a ritual procedure in Lao folk medicine to entice the *khouan,* or soul controlling a particular bodily function, to return to the body.[17]

Another reward comes from just being, learning, and playing together, which confirms their concept of a more embracing humanity. One core member of a sponsorship committee wrote this letter to her small-town newspaper eleven days after the arrival of a Laotian family to describe her joy:

> It would be an understatement to say that this committee has worked hard. I found it a personal pleasure to work with every member. But the best and most rewarding day I had, and I will treasure it forever, occurred three days after their arrival. . . . We hit upon the idea of a soccer ball and secured one. In the meantime I picked up my son and two of his friends from school and went back to "our family's house" for a few minutes. I told the children to play outside while I tended to something inside. After a few minutes, I looked outside and saw three Americans and three Laotians kicking that soccer ball all over the place laughing, falling, shouting, and talking in two different languages and having a lot of fun. . . . Later, at dinner, my husband and I asked, trying to be very casual, how the children were able to communicate. My son replied easily, "I don't know, we just understood each other."

> I hope we can learn something from these children. This [December] is a time of year when everyone's sense of love and brotherhood is heightened and I hope we remember it throughout the new year. I am thankful that this lovely family has been brought to us. My belief in the brotherhood of all men, and the need for love and compassion has been renewed. I needed that reassurance right now. This family is a wonderful Christmas present.

The leaders all said response within their churches to the refugees had been warm and positive; sponsorship was also sometimes said to have induced greater cohesion within the church. The only instance of criticism was evoked by a leader putting a notice in the church newsletter soliciting a color television set for the refugees. Leaders of the interfaith committees said the responses in their churches was overwhelmingly positive.

Community response was also predominantly positive. One minister (not in a sponsorship in the sample) who had been fearful of popular response because of his observations of racist attitudes in town, noted that he had been "pleasantly surprised" at the positive response. Some individual acts of discrimination such as refusal to rent to the refugees were remarked on by leaders. Some leaders were aware of covert rumbling of verbal opposition, but it was not expressed to them, so the number of critics and their status in the community could not be pinpointed. Rumblings were channeled to the clergy by their invitation in the above cases. There was no overt expression of negative opinion voiced in any media. The media, often highlighting human-interest stories about refugees and interviews about the project, were usually very positive toward sponsorship.

The interfaith committees also seemed to evoke a broad solidarity in their towns. Several leaders of such committees talked of how much they had enjoyed working with people they had not known before. However, in the two cases where the communities succeeded, structures for interfaith cooperation had existed earlier.

Thus, leaders of sponsoring committees were rewarded by fulfilling their own values, by "doing the Lord's work," by confirming and enhancing their self-image, by seeing the impact of their collective act, and by enjoying the friendship of the refugees (no longer strangers) who reciprocated their concern.

The assumptions and rewards of sponsors interviewed are similar to those of voluntary blood donors remarked upon by Titmuss:

> Practically all the voluntary donors whose answers we set down in their own words employed a moral vocabulary to explain their reasons for giving blood. . . . For most of them the universe was not limited and confined to the family, the kinship, or to a defined social, ethnic or occupational group or class; it was the universal stranger. . . . None of the donors' answers was purely altruistic. . . . There must be some feeling of obligation, approval and interest, some feeling of "inclusion" in society: some awareness of need and the purposes of the gift.[18]

The lack of any comparable experience was commented on by a few leaders. Frank Myerhof, who had begun as a follower (initially skeptical about the mobilizers' ability to carry it off), wanted to do more. He recalled how his committee had considered at one point remaining together and converting the group to a "burnout squad" to help victims of fires or disasters. "We went to the minister but he said there was no need for it," he recalled with a hint of dismay. At last report, his committee was sponsoring a third refugee family, relatives of their first family who had just been located in the camps.

5

Conclusions and Implications

Expectations and Findings

LOOKING back on expectations drawn from the literature on collectivities helping victims to evade persecution, it was proposed that three processes had to occur for helping to become the rule. First, the victims must be seen and potential helpers must recognize them as innocent victims and include them within their universe of obligation. Second, moral leaders within congregations and communities must acknowledge their responsibility and ability to help. Third, support should be mobilized along the lines of preexisting social organization and networks by appealing to the group's values and norms. In the case of refugee sponsorship, it was anticipated that voluntary support would snowball once sponsorship was legitimated by the congregation and the norm of helpfulness was evoked. The questions examined herein pertain to how sponsorships were started, the role of clergy and laity in leadership, the role of public opinion within the church, the characteristics of leaders, instigators, and models acting on them, and the presence or absence of rational cost appraisal in deciding whether to sponsor refugees.

The expectations proposed proved to be correct. The "boat-people" were highly visible before the project began. Few potential sponsors questioned whether they were innocent victims. The immediate recognition of their plight and empathy with them was experienced individually at first in response to the media depiction of them as innocent victims in a dramatic life-threatening situation not of their own making. The boat-people became emblematic of all the Indochinese refugees (and later, the starving Cambodians). Yet such transitory feeling had no impact in itself on a single enthusiast or mobilizer of sponsorship interviewed; none was moved to sponsor as an individual or to explore group sponsorship by the media. (This is not a critique of the media, for the first question on the national agenda was taking in more refugees. It is not known whether the media could have mobilized such demand had they portrayed sponsorship as a way to help. A media campaign by one agency for foster-parents for unaccompanied minors among the refugees and coincident false rumors about the availability of Cambodian children for adoption did generate many phone calls to me as a sponsorship developer—and presumably, many to the agency—but one does not know whether to relate this to a desire to help refugees or to the unsatisfied public demand for adoptable children.) Few people volunteered to sponsor in the entire county without group support, and two of the four individual sponsors known to me became aware of sponsorship as a result of the sponsorship development project of the RIC.

Every case of sponsorship depended on the initiative of one (or more) enthusiast(s) embedded in the core of the church who acknowledged personal responsibility to help the refugees, attracted others (always a minority), and put the question on the church agenda, prodding the decision-making body or authority in the church to approve it. In a minority of sponsorships, ministers were the first enthusiasts. When clergy became enthusiasts—and this constituted a small minority of all clergy—they needed the prior approval of the laity in non–Roman Catholic churches, except for the instances where ministeria themselves sponsored. Almost all known cases of clergy who became enthusiasts were successful in attracting lay support. Clergy support was almost exclusively drawn from congregations in main-line denominations in which social action was accepted as normative. Differences among types of denominations and their constituencies affected the likelihood of enthusiasts emerging and expecting a receptive audience and clergy support. Evangelical and funda-mentalist churches who have been traditionally concerned first with salva-tion of souls scarcely ever considered sponsorship or sponsored in Riverside County.

Besides appeals from their own denominations, enthusiasts were influ-enced by local organizations crosscutting denominations, directly by the RIC and indirectly by the IAW. The RIC offered potential sponsors tangi-ble guidance in mobilizing support in their congregations and organizing the sponsorship itself. Both organizations put potential sponsors in con-tact with others of similar backgrounds who had sponsored and served as role models, reinforcing their inclination to become involved. Subsequent experience showed the limits to when and how much community organiza-tions, the churches, and the nationwide Volags could mobilize participa-tion, as exhibited in the campaign for Cuban sponsors (later discussed); the public must first agree that these are innocent victims before coming to their aid.

The enthusiasts are alike in their self-consciousness that they really are their brothers' keepers. Some would express their motives in terms of the idea of mission, rescuing and resettling refugees being an act of sacra-ment—"doing the Lord's work." Others put it simply in terms of helping people in need, responding to one's neighbor, "doing what had to be done." Enthusiasts were likely to be drawn from the more educated strata of the population, people in midlife with an established career and family. They were likely (if male) to be professional and technical workers in knowledge industries and (if female) to be out of the labor force or working part-time in schools, services, and the nonprofit sector. They are predominantly white, nativeborn, and belong to nonethnic churches in main-line denominations. They are immersed in the church as a com-munity and association, and church membership is (for the mobilizers) usually their most engaging civic activity. Apart from this, they share few attributes in common.

While the earliest congregations to become committed to sponsorship appeared to share a sense of crisis and spent little time in coming to a commitment, once the public awareness of the Indochinese situation as a crisis diminished (a product of both the media and the number of crises in 1979–80), the appeal for sponsorship was treated neither as a routinized request for charity nor as an emergency demanding response. The ref-ugees who were to be sponsored were, after all, then in camps protected by the UN High Commissioner of Refugees, and while they were living amid great overcrowding and appalling sanitary conditions, they were not in immediate danger. In the northeast one could always imagine alternatives for resettlement in summer climates (like California), which would appeal more to the refugees (as it did). Most often, sponsorship was conceived of as an optional project or act of mission.

Expression of public opinion within the churches appears to be shaped by the churches' own imperatives and assumptions. Only in a minority of cases was ideological opposition (defending the position that "we" as a nation, class, race, or ethnic group have no obligation to divert resources to refugees) publicly voiced and in every case know about, it was defeated. Once sponsorship was put on the agenda of the congregation and a minimal core of supporters had come forth, the governing body or au-thority of the church had either to affirm or deny their own values as their brothers' keeper in its decision-making process. To deny them would negate their self-conception and cause discomfort or cognitive dissonance.[1] Therefore, sponsorship as a worthy *objective* was never repudiated; if a congregation rejected sponsorship, it denied that it had the ability to achieve that objective by negatively appraising its resources. This is not to imply that their explanations were simply rationalizations.

In every instance in which a congregation had considered sponsorship but had not sponsored, I called them (in my role as a sponsorship developer) to inquire what had happened. Rejections were usually attributed to (1) simple lack of resources or volunteers, (2) previous social commitments of the congregation that drained the free time of active members, (3) organizational problems of the congregation (often the absence or expected turnover of a minister) negating any new commitments, or (4) lack of resources in the area to meet needs of refugees. In three cases out of five, it was approved. It is not known if or how enthusiasts appraised costs (but some valued benefits), but congregations ordinarily did. (One cannot tell from the data presented, but such appraisal was more likely in 1980 than in 1979.) Enthusiasts in congregations with resistance may also have put the question on the church agenda later when there was lesser awareness of a crisis so there was more time and inclination for such appraisal.) The Sponsorship Development Project of the RIC which began in September 1979, also attracted and created new enthusiasts who then went back to congregations whose members saw nightly on their television sets the emaciated victims of an appalling famine in Cambodia, the specter of American impotence in the Iranian hostage situation, and flotillas of Cuban refugees arriving here. The growth of unemployment, inflation, and perceptions of an endless chain of demands for aid may have increased consciousness of costs and a collective sense of being pressed.

Once approved by the congregation (or governing authority), support for sponsorship usually snowballed within the church—the norm of helpfulness was evoked as expected. Just as congregants would put a bill in the collection plate for a church appeal for the bishop's fund, for a local family without insurance that had a fire, or for world hunger, they would make a donation for sponsorship. The plethora of used clothing and furniture ordinarily collected for rummage sales meant churches had an in-built resource base to set up an apartment and clothe a family. More important were the networks of people used to working together, to meeting weekly, to sharing values and traditions. The networks of associations within the church encouraged more participation: teenagers could put on dance-a-thons, the women's guild put on crafts sales, and so on. The unorganized community response was usually predominantly positive. Once present and real, the refugees evoked more identification and helpfulness usually.

What was unexpected was the virtually unanimous agreement on the rewards to the sponsor, which exceeded, sponsors felt, what they had given notwithstanding the time they had spent and the problems they experienced. These rewards flow from the bond between sponsor and refugee first formed vicariously by the sponsor prior to the refugees' arrival. The refugee-sponsor bond, although stemming from a novel social encounter, is an example of how the norm of reciprocity elicits mutual affect and caring in a relationship starting out with one-way giving.

The Paradox of Defining Altruism

The question of rewards returns one to the old controversy about altruism and may clarify the problem. Some would say (and have said for centuries) that the sponsors' identification is an extension of egotism and their enjoyment of the refugees is an act of psychic exploitation.

But, does not this criticism assume that doing good should be without affect or joy? Or could it be, as John Clarke recognized in 1605, that "the benevolent man . . . is merely a man who happens to find his happiness in the happiness of others."[2] Lifesaving especially leads to a unique joy. Aage Bertelsen, leader of a Danish resistance ring that ferried Jews hunted by the German Gestapo to Sweden in 1943, recalls an

> . . . almost too intense feeling of happiness, which seemed to me to be entirely different from all other emotional experiences. I was walking beside Dr. Strandbygaard [another helper in the ring]. Suddenly she said, "Isn't this strange? Don't you think so? A very strange feeling! It's almost like experiencing again the overwhelming love of one's youth."
>
> . . . the whole atmosphere of the beach up there rested like a blessing on the relief work, and on the rooms in Buddinge Lane. . . . We agreed that no matter what might happen to us we could not have done without that period.
>
> "No, because it's like this," said Gerda [Mrs. Bertelsen] very quietly, "it's as if we never realized before what it means to live."[3]

The paradox of altruism if defined conventionally by the absence of any rewards—vicarious enjoyment, reciprocal sympathy, feeling good about one's giving, the other, and the self—is that the examples usually negate the definition, leaving one with an empty theoretical classification. Aronfreed, on the other hand, limited the "concept of altruism . . . to the choice of an act which is at least partly determined by the actor's expectation of consequences which will benefit another person without benefit to himself . . . not necessarily without objective (and reinforcement) value for the actor."[4]

Further, even identification with the other as other tends to be a self-annulling motive in an altruistic transaction such as refugee sponsorship, for as one begins to identify with the refugee and internalizes the role of the other(s), he or she is no longer perceived as the other but simply as a fellow human. To relate to a person as an other 'differentiated by race, ethnicity, nationality, or religion' is to objectify the person, but one cannot identify with and objectify people at the same time. Once one takes the role of the other, helping refugees becomes just a case of helping a relative or newfound friend caught in an unusual situation—homeless and stateless. They then become symbolic kin or "one of us." Those who began with an all-embracing concept and commitment to a religious or humanistic conception of universality, such as Arthur Brown, saw this at once. Arthur recalled that:

> Some people would say, "Why not take care of our own people?" What they didn't understand, I told them, was that in the Lord's eyes these are our own people.

How people learn who they are and develop conscience and commitments by identification, by taking the role and percepts of the other, and by moral and cognitive development, is a question addressed by diverse theorists, including Sigmund Freud, George Herbert Mead, Charles Horton Cooley, and Lawrence Kohlberg. Their explanations readily comprehend how and why people identify with and internalize the rules of those to whom they belong, whom they depend upon, and who are more powerful than they are. But sympathetic identification or empathy with those less powerful and different is also a product of social learning in part. That such sympathy can not be reduced to simple self-interest was remarked upon over two centuries ago by Adam Smith in *The Theory of Moral Sentiments* (1759):

> Sympathy, however, cannot, in any sense be regarded as a selfish principle . . . though sympathy is very properly said to arise from an imaginary change of situations with the person principally concerned, yet this imaginary change is not supposed to happen to me in my own person, and character, but in that of the person with whom I sympathize. . . . My grief, therefore, is entirely upon your account, and not in the least upon my own. It is not, therefore, in the least selfish. . . . A man may sympathize with a woman in childbed; though it is impossible that he should conceive himself as suffering her pains in his own proper person and character. That whole account of human nature, however, which deduces all sentiments and affections from self-love, which has made so much noise in the world, but which, so far as I know, has never yet been fully and distinctly explained, seems to me to have arisen from some confused misapprehension of the system of sympathy.[5]

Rewards flow from acting upon sympathy. With direct experience of the other, sympathy becomes empathy. As empathy expands and sponsors become godparents, they vicariously enjoyed their refugees' growth, vitality, and transformation—a child playing ball, a young woman walking to work smiling and confident, a family sitting down to dinner at their own table. This intensity of feeling is not compatible with easy adaptation to the end of a transient role. (In fact, it may make it worse because the guilt the godparents' identification instigates in the refugees may make the latter postpone telling sponsors about their plans for departure until the very last moment.)

Two explanations were advanced for this sense of loss, bitterness, and grief that sometimes was expressed among sponsors when refugees left before they became autonomous (or before their autonomy is accepted). However, these occurred among a minority of cases in which refugees moved. The acceptance of change among the majority was attributed to the leaders' anticipation and preparation for this as a possible and legitimate choice of the refugees.

The test of exploitation is not whether sponsors derive pleasure or self-satisfaction from the sponsorship but whether the helper's needs or interests are put before that of the refugee and conflict with their interests. Put more generally, one may ask: Do the helper's acts really enable, or do they disable, the one helped? Does the sponsor help the refugees to become self-reliant and "at home" in a new land, or are the refugees patronized and indulged for the psychic gratification of the sponsor (prolonging their dependency) or exploited as a source of labor or a convert to the faith?

Evaluation of Sponsorships in Riverside County

Examined in terms of these criteria, the Riverside County congregational sponsorships were successful. Most leaders consistently tried to understand and put the refugees' interests before their interests.

All but one planned sponsorship was successful in bringing the refugees to Riverside County by that committee; a constituent congregation also took over the sponsorship in the case of the interfaith committee that dissolved. In eighteen of the nineteen sponsorships, sponsors and refugees succeeded at achieving a consensus on the goal of the relationship.

The commitment to support the refugees and enable them to become autonomous was sustained in every case—despite problems and occasionally tensions—as long as the refugees stayed in Riverside County. There were no defections among congregational sponsors. Based on reports of other sponsorship developers and Volag representatives, it appears that such constancy is typical of congregational sponsors. By contrast, 5 percent of individual sponsors of Cuban refugees were reported to have cast them out in 1980; it may be that this is not only a reflection on differences in the bonds between congregational and individual sponsors but on the motivation of the Cuban refugee-sponsors and the haste and lack of selectivity in choosing them.[6]

In terms of adaptation, refugees sponsored by the congregations whom I studied who remained in Riverside County for more than nine months were more likely to be self-supporting than Indochinese refugees in other parts of the United States. No instance of exploitation of refugees as workers or servants in a family business or personal household of a sponsor was observed. All but one refugee family in the study (and that was the most recently arrived refugee) had at least one member employed, and only one of the eighty-one refugees (1 percent) sponsored by the sample study received cash assistance in the county at the time of the study. Indeed, if I include all the Indochinese refugees arriving in Riverside County between 1979 and 1981, I would estimate that a maximum of 5 to 8 percent of them received cash assistance during that period in the county. By contrast, the great increase in the numbers of refugees elsewhere in the United States dependent on welfare caused growing concern among officials during this period.

Surveys of the dependency of Indochinese refugees on cash assistance in 1980 and 1981 show that from 45 percent to 67 percent of the refugees claimed cash assistance; variations in the reported rate are related to the areas sampled, definition of terms of computation, and the inclusion of other (non-Indochinese) refugees—principally Cubans—in the highest estimate.[7] Similarly, a systematic study of a sample of congregational sponsors in 1983 showed 38 percent of refugees arriving in fiscal year 1980 had depended on full cash assistance and 34 percent on supplemental cash assistance at some time; however, only 7 percent of the 1980 refugees were recipients of full and 7 percent of supplemental cash assistance at the time of study (1983), according to sponsor reports. The longer refugees have been in the United States, the more likely they are to be self-sufficient and employed—as were three of every four Church World Services–sponsored refugees who arrived in 1980 by 1983, according to the CWS study—and the less likely they are to use public assistance. That study also found that 86 percent of refugee families arriving in 1980 had at least one member employed in 1983; similarly, a federal study found that 79 percent of 1980 Indochinese refugees in the labor force were employed in 1983.[8] I cannot infer to what extent my findings can be attributed to the relatively few refugees and low unemployment in Riverside County, to the transmission of sponsors' values, to their strategy, or to the interaction of all these factors. Nor can I assess whether congregationally sponsored refugees are less likely to be dependent on cash assistance than are other refugees because the little data that has been classified by the sponsoring Volag do not discriminate between the formal sponsor—the Volag—and the actual resettlement agent with whom the refugee has most contact: a local agency, a congregation, or a family—relatives of the Indochinese or unrelated Americans. Volags that concentrate on congregational sponsorship also process sponsorships by relatives with some or little participation by a neighboring congregation. One survey of Vietnamese refugees arriving in 1975 did show that the refugees sponsored by Volags relying predominantly on congregational sponsorships were half (or less) as likely to be receiving cash assistance than refugees sponsored by two of the other three Volags reported. But surveys from 1981 on the use of cash assistance by refugees in areas with high concentrations of refugees, classifying refugees by the sponsoring Volag, do not show a consistent pattern.[9]

To be sure, autonomy or self-support is only one index of adaptation. This study is inadequate to assess the latent effects of congregational sponsorship on the refugees, nor does it compare it to other models of sponsorship. The refugees were not interviewed, although a Vietnamese priest and a refugee from the 1975 cohort who had been a confidante (and relative of some) of the newer refugees were interviewed. During the period of sponsorship, I had heard from (and about) refugees who had indirect means of registering dissatisfaction with sponsors. While complaints from sponsors and refugees in individual sponsorships were frequent, complaints from either or both parties in group sponsorships were much less common.

The Indochinese refugees resettled and remaining in Riverside County appear to be both getting ahead in terms of their own goals while retaining some sense of who they are collectively and becoming more cohesive as a community. Members of four (of fourteen) Indochinese refugee households of sampled sponsors still residing in the county were enrolled in advanced English courses, community college programs, or apprenticeship training courses in 1982. Formal and informal ethnic organizations and informal support groups and networks have developed. The Vietnamese have an independent community association, and the Lao families have regular social get-togethers, sometimes on their initiative and sometimes planned by sponsors. Refugees of the same group from adjacent counties often attended such gatherings. From a number of perspectives, this seems to have been a successful example of resettlement, taking into account the movement that may be expected due to secondary migration.

Furthermore, no negative responses by the community nor ethnic or class tensions have been reported in contrast to other communities. However, one must note that negative reports usually come from communities in which refugees were resettled in large numbers or in which they constituted a sizable percent of the population and/or were seen to be in competition with other ethnic groups. None of these conditions characterize Riverside County.

Comparative Evaluation of Models of Resettlement

One may question whether the impact of congregational or group sponsorship differs from that of other models of sponsorship. Despite the millions being spent on resettlement of refugees, there has been scarcely any evaluation of the effects of models of resettlement for the refugees and the public. These include bureaucratic processing of refugees by social workers with or without the assistance of ethnic aides, relative and other private sponsorships, and simply channeling refugees onto the welfare rolls without providing them either a sense of relationship or social services as well as congregational sponsorship. There has been criticism of the inadequacy of some of the Volags' follow-up and conception of services but little research as to the impact of such models and strategies on the refugees and on the public.[10] Most studies of the adjustment of refugees focus on the impact of characteristics and achievements of the refugees disregarding their experiences during flight and resettlement. Taking this design bias of existent research into account, one finds several related questions: What is (1) the impact of congregational sponsorship on refugees' employment and level of employment; (2) the impact of English communication skills on employability; (3) the impact of congregational sponsorship by English speakers on the English learning of Indochinese refugees; (4) the effects of both employment and English communication skills on the refugees' general adjustment; and (5) the latent dysfunctions of sponsorship on refugees versus the expected positive consequences. Several arguments have emerged based on limited evidence.

Sponsors have been accused by Kelly of having a short-term approach to employment, channeling the Indochinese into the lower-class dead-end jobs (because of the sponsors' limited funds) without giving them an opportunity for language and job retraining.[11] A Canadian study found that although sponsors did insure that their Indochinese refugees received language training, this was insufficient to prevent downward mobility and concluded:

> In their role as social facilitators, sponsors, with few exceptions, adopted a strictly instrumental and short-term approach. They tried to make the refugees self-sufficient as soon as language training was completed and helped them in locating whatever work happened to be available, sometimes with the promise to look for better paying jobs.[12]

In the United States, Vietnamese refugees were half as likely to find white-collar jobs as they had been in Vietnam, but by many reports, they are an upwardly mobile group, intent on education, and drawn toward finding niches in technologically innovative and expanding fields, such as electronics and computers.[13] Kelly's criticism conceals several assumptions: first, the downward mobility that the refugees experienced could have been prevented and they were entitled to expect to start at a higher level; second, there is a good or perfect relationship between English skills and employment or wage level; and third, that education and employment are necessarily separate phases. The first assumption is not only empirically questionable but raises questions of social ethics and equity; in a multiethnic society with a high rate of unemployment amid groups that have been here for centuries, her assumption that refugees have a right to begin to compete on a higher level will attract little support.

The question is: at what level should refugees expect (and be supported and prepared) to start? Regarding the goals of sponsors, the Volags usually take the position that the sponsors' responsibility is to give the refugees a start, not to guarantee their destination. Sponsors can be encouraged to look for the most suitable starting job, given a refugee's training, skills, and future contribution, and the labor-market situation. But the responsibility of planning and sacrificing toward that future is not that of the sponsors primarily unless they undertake that willingly. Perhaps both sponsors and refugees need a two-track orientation toward both employment and education, accepting the need to start at one level and make gradual phased progress toward longer-term goals, realizing that their need for English will expand with their need to express themselves; a recent survey of sponsors and refugees shows that both agree on this need.[14] One might then expect that as refugees became self-supporting and plan toward new aspirations, their ability and motivation to learn English would increase. Thus, the tension aroused by poorly paid and nonfulfilling work might be used to arouse them to plan toward future goals, mitigating the more depressing effects of work on immediate morale.

There is no evidence as to whether the level of employment attained by refugees sponsored by congregations differs from that attained by other refugees. There has been continuing controversy among officials and service-providers concerned with refugees whether to emphasize the need for immediate (or speedy) employment or invest in saturating refugees with ESL and vocational retraining initially, as some nations do, requiring prolonged dependency. English communication skills are valued positively by sponsors, refugees, and planners for their impact on the employability of refugees, which, along with communication, affects their general adjustment; to be able to communicate is essential to feel good about oneself, and to have a job is to be deemed socially competent and valued and enables one to be independent.[15] While refugees are less likely to find and keep jobs if they cannot communicate or understand little English, there is an imperfect relation between English skills and employment, and other variables may be as or more important in predicting whether they find work.[16] Refugees who can communicate little, or not at all, are unlikely to find work, but above minimal competency, there is scant relationship between communication skills and employability. Because the government planners do not anticipate being able to support refugees for the time needed to achieve mastery of English and wish to discourage prolonged dependency, officially sponsored and supported ESL programs usually stress "survival English."[17]

There is no evidence of the impact of different resettlement strategies— congregational sponsorship, relative sponsorship, and social-work institutional processing—on learning English, but some evidence exists that Southeast Asian refugees have more difficulty learning English than do refugees from European-language backgrounds and that sponsors of the same nationality (usually relatives) as refugees are likely to retard the development of refugees' English-language skills.[18] English-speaking sponsors may motivate refugees to talk and provide encounters where conversation can be practiced informally.

A more controversial question (often concealed) is what refugees should expect or get. The most frequent complaint is not of the level but of the disparity of benefits; one Canadian study showed that refugees themselves were not primarily dissatisfied with the material differences in benefits if they trusted their sponsor.[19]

But refugees do not live by bread alone. The need for community, to share their scarred past with other survivors and to re-create the institutions of daily life that require some ethnic concentration, is a need most refugees fleeing from life-threatening situations have shown. One must also ask whether personal dignity of refugees is enhanced or diminished by the processes of resettlement and relationships with sponsors and/or agencies involved.

Several researchers have pointed to the potentially negative effects of sponsorship in dispersing the refugees, depriving them of the benefits of ethnic community, and prompting frequent secondary migration. Sponsors may also initially place refugees in housing in their neighborhoods, that the latter cannot afford over the long term, causing them to have unrealistic expectations. Moreover, American sponsors may unintentionally reinforce the dependency of the Indochinese refugees. Montero observes:

> The Vietnamese next entered a period in which they are assigned to a private sponsor who pledges personal and financial support to the refugee families.

> From one perspective, this sponsorship period serves to disperse the Viet-
> namese to the four winds and deprives them of the social and psychological
> comfort of their ethnic community. From another perspective, this sponsorship
> period may provide a degree of American social contact and economic security,
> unknown to earlier Asian immigrants, which accelerated the pace of their
> assimilation.[20]

Many questions are involved. Do middle-class white Americans provide realistic models for comparison and emulation for refugees who will become one of many Asian minorities in the United States? Are refugees involved in such sponsorships more likely to repudiate their cultural identity prematurely and assimilate superficially? Are refugees more able to interpret and accept their own feelings of loss, depression, and lone-liness during the second stage of resettlement if guided by others from the same ethnic group who have undergone similar experiences recently?[21] Do majority-group guides tend to be paternalistic tutors, taking over decision making, or can they be guided to become friends and mentors, enabling the refugee to become autonomous? Do other refugees afford each other a compensating sense of community or does that security enable them to be better able to avoid the work—and often pain—associated with learning a new language and survival skills?

Although many studies of adjustment note the symptoms of the Indo-chinese refugees associated with their losses—mourning, loss, and guilt for those dead and separated family members[22]—Starr and Roberts observe how adept such refugees are in coping and the importance of community contexts and fit between self and community in predicting adjustment.[23] Sponsors' sensitivity to such problems may be raised by the involvement of longer-settled Indochinese refugees in resettlement. Sponsors' self-criticism (discussed previously herein) suggests that sponsorship can become a more sophisticated, reflective practice, using guidance and resources from the previously resettled refugees, the Volags and government agencies, as well as organized self-help. Because of its visibility and high level of involvement, the pitfalls of sponsorship become more apparent than that of other modes of resettlement.

The government is also responsible for the oversight of the Volags to ensure that their sponsors do not exploit the relation to propagate their own goals through proselytism—conversion of the refugees to a new religion—as some sponsors of one evangelical Volag (not included in this study) have done.[24] Although this has not been a frequent complaint of refugees, it is a means of coercive assimilation, stripping of identity.

The question of the impact of congregational sponsorship is confounded by the contexts of sponsorship; this stems from the original government policy of resettling refugees for the greatest dispersion, depriving them of others of the same background. It seemed clear that dense Indochinese concentrations, reinforced by secondary migration, were apt to lead to intergroup competition for jobs, housing, and resources as they did on the Gulf Coast and major western cities, occasionally leading to violent incidents. Yet other Indochinese ethnic concentrations proved to be stable and coexisted productively in pluralistic communities. The official policy of dispersion was countered by the spontaneous remigration of the Vietnamese toward concentrations in California and the Sunbelt that repeated the movement of other Asian minorities in the past. Given the rapid unfolding of the crisis in Indochina during 1979, it is not surprising planners neglected to look at historical experiences which indicate some limits on planning.

Defining Collective Altruism

The refugee crisis of 1979 in southeast Asia provoked the need for both lifesaving and collective altruism. Lifesaving is a response to an emergency, aroused without premeditation, by the immediate recognition that the victim will die unless one intervenes now. Once the Indochinese situation was stabilized by international agreement to take in more refugees from nations of first asylum and Vietnam agreed to halt the coercion that led to the exodus, the focus was on the refugee camps and the plight of refugees was less likely to be seen as desperate—ashore and encamped, they did not need lifesaving. Thus, for the congregations asked to sponsor the Indochinese refugees, the act called for was an act of collective altruism, a normative option—a good thing to do competing with other good things to do. The enthusiasts who mobilized these congregations need not have been autonomous altruists, for their way of helping was approved, enabled, and funded by colleagues, coworkers, congregants, church, and state.

When the cost of the aftermath of lifesaving adds up—for saved victims must be fed and housed rather than mourned—the question of national and international responsibility emerges. Thus, collective altruism is best defined on the level of public or group policy rather than individual motivation or behavior. One may label the policy of a collectivity—whether it is a government, an association, or a congregation—as altruistic insofar as it benefits people who are not members of the collectivity and the collectivity has limited resources. Individuals may help, contribute, desist from, or avoid involvement; they may be moved by their conception of duty whether it is religious or secular), by their identification with the victim or beneficiary, their identification with the group that supports such a policy, by their fear of censure for not giving, or by enjoyment of giving of themselves, or by all these things. Nonaltruistic motives may reinforce altruistic ends, and altruistic behavior may be evoked from people who reject altruism once helping becomes the normative thing to do. So, there are walks for hunger that make money by having walkers solicit sponsors to pay them for the length of their performance and engender competition among walkers; there funds for the disabled that grant contributors national publicity on television in staged events; further people are invited by newly formed "foundations" and "institutes" to become "fellows" in return for a generous contribution and may emblazon their names on the foundation block of colleges and hospitals by paying for them.

Voluntarism and Public Responsibility

In terms of future policy, the evidence that congregational sponsorship enlarges public participation in and support for refugee resettlement could be used to extend the possibility for bringing in more refugees in the United States (as it might have been—but was not—in Canada) during the Indochinese crisis.[25] There is tentative evidence from Canadian experiences that "individuals who sponsor out of spontaneous goodwill for reasons of personal growth are much less likely to follow through on their responsibilities than those who sponsor from a feeling of moral obligation based on religious or humanitarian principles."[26] Moreover, better organized groups with preexistent affiliation, such as church groups, were better organized and more cohesive. Thus, congregations are a natural and reliable basis on which to organize help to strangers to start new lives.[27]

But can one rely on voluntarism to fulfill public policy? One proposal to shift all responsibility for refugee resettlement to the community-based voluntary agencies (including the larger bureaucratic fund-raising agencies), which was rejected within the federal bureaucracy, was repudiated by the U.S. Coordinator for Refugee Affairs on the grounds that the voluntary agencies would never assume sole financial responsibility, that most of these agencies had no experience in refugee resettlement, that refugee resettlement had been federalized by statute, and that dependency was intrinsic and inevitable to this process:

> With the enormous increase in U.S. resettlement flows resulting from the exodus from Indochina, public assistance has become a fixture in the resettlement process. Refugees now enter the country with a sophisticated understanding of the assistance programs available to them and are routinely steered to the welfare office shortly after their arrival. The result is that an increasing proportion of the refugee population—particularly the Indochinese—is involved with the welfare culture, creating growing dependency, tensions with community groups, and high costs for the taxpayer.[28]

This study indicates that prolonged dependency and immersion in the welfare culture is not an inevitable result of resettlement but may be partly attributable to the type of sponsorship and resettlement strategy. Yet the congregations who volunteered conceived of their help in most cases as a complement, not a substitute, to federal commitment and aid. The sponsors also acknowledged their sense of entitlement to use the system, drawn by the benefits, the relationship of benefits, and the irrationality of the American system, which provides disincentives to the working poor. First, one must recall that the congregational volunteers responded to the U.S. public commitment to refugees, which was both an incentive and a back-up: they accepted sponsorship with the assurance that they were not financially responsible for the refugees although most raised substantial resources. Most sponsors claimed food stamps and Medicaid as entitlements for refugees, conceiving food and medical care as basic needs. Since virtually all sponsors had ample medical insurance, the lack of insurance for refugees whether or not they were employed (for the kind of jobs they got seldom had any benefits) troubled most of them. But qualifying for Medicaid (during that period) meant automatically qualifying for cash assistance. (This has been changed since that time.)

Another conflict for refugees created by the system was that between working and improving one's skills to get ahead in the future. Virtually all vocational training and ESL immersion programs in the county then were restricted to the unemployed (by U. S. law) so that working refugees who needed more training or language skills could not enroll, providing another incentive to becoming unemployed and claiming public assistance. Since most sponsors had followed Father Paul's initial advice to support the refugees in an immersion and training program for six months (although some refugees preferred to, and did, get jobs earlier), this was not a problem for many.

Does the widespread experience of refugee sponsorship, one may ask, enable the government, were it willing to do so, to make a greater commitment toward refugees seeking entry to the United States? Can the government through the Volags draw upon experienced refugee sponsors as a resource? When asked about their willingness to become involved in sponsorship again, the leaders of Riverside County Committees interviewed were divided. Two-thirds were willing, but half of these would not act as chair or coordinator because of the drain on their time; the others were uncertain or just could not contemplate another commitment at the moment. In fact, half of the fourteen committees studied had sponsored or were expecting a second or third household. Their response (looking toward the future) slightly exceeds the proportion of 1975 sponsors in Riverside County sponsoring in 1979–80. In both cases, sponsors had learned to appraise the costs first. This seems to me to point to a growing reservoir of experienced sponsors whose energy can be drawn on in an international emergency (providing they perceive it as an emergency and identify with the victim as an innocent victim). This reinforces the need to fairly enforce the Refugee Act of 1980, which identifies political refugees in accordance with the definition of the U.N. and consistently discriminates political from economic refugees—without bias but with mercy. Failure to do so would also raise serious questions of equity among potential entrants to the United States, given the limits on immigration and the intense competition.

It appears that the supply of congregational sponsors may be an index of the correspondence between public policy and popular consensus that a category of refugees are innocent victims. It seems probable that it will need to be supplemented by other means of resettlement, for congregants may not agree on the definition of the victims, may not acknowledge their responsibility toward them, or may deny they have the resources to help them. Furthermore, the demand by sponsors for refugees and the supply of refugees may be in disequilibrium; not only because of variations in the flow of refugees (and of the interest of sponsors), but because of differences in the geographical distribution of sponsors and refugees' geographical preferences for resettlement.

Public Responses to Refugees and Needy Others

Were the reception of refugees dependent solely on public voluntary support or collective altruism, one may inquire what effects this might have. Insofar as giving is a democratic group decision, groups assess their resources, costs, their relative needs, and the level of material well-being when weighing commitments. (Similar questions, of course, emerge among official representatives of the public in weighing allocations.) Assuming (in order to develop theoretical expectations) that the perception of the refugees as innocent victims is constant, if giving is related to people's sense of well-being (as was observed among sponsorship leaders), the more deprived the members of a group felt, the less apt they would be to share with others. But feelings of deprivation are not only caused by a lack of money or goods but by comparison with others: one may feel inferior because others with like characteristics get more, attributing one's state to inequity. If some of the homeless are given a new home because of the particular cause of their homelessness and others are not, feelings of deprivation and resentment would be expected. Thus, one would expect the readiness to take in refugees would be inversely related to the prevalence of feelings of deprivation in comparison to them: the more people feel themselves deprived, the less they will do for others. The relative lack of resources and public concern for the welfare of the poor, the unemployed, and the homeless that is public policy at the time of writing (1983) as compared to an official administrative and legislative commitment (albeit scarcely voiced) for homeless refugees might well reinforce feelings of deprivation among poorer Americans and unemployed and homeless Americans. From this, it follows that the greater the sense of inequity there is stemming from the lack of compassion in domestic allotments, the less empathy there would be and willingness to share with groups outside the polity. If donors democratically elect who will be the beneficiaries, it is not only the level of wealth or surplus income available for charity that conditions their choices but their self-appraisal of deprivation and their collective appraisal of relative needs. This implies the need for an integrated approach toward planning for the welfare of one's own constituency and of refugees for both the sake of equity and the political viability of refugee programs. The legitimation of sponsorship depends on public affirmation that we are responsible for our neighbors here also.

U.S. Official and Public Discrimination among Refugees

Another variable relating to public willingness to sponsor refugees is the characteristics, motives, and perception of the refugees themselves. Many of the denominational Volags appeal for sponsors in the name of the abstract universal refugee both for religious reasons (disdaining ethnic or political discriminations) and in order to routinize the supply of sponsors; as one denominational Volag sponsorship developer put it: "We take our refugees from the menu of the day." Yet, there is no evidence of a generalized response to refugees as an abstract type. One can see this vividly by comparing the public and congregational response to the Cuban influx in 1980 (first labeled as illegal and then welcomed by President Carter) in comparison to the response to the Indochinese refugees in 1979–80. Conversations with sponsorship developers and staff of different Volags showed that potential congregational sponsors' response to the Cubans was the same in all denominations: they refused to sponsor them regardless of how much effort the Volags put in to develop sponsors. (This also applies to the sponsors of Indochinese refugees in our sample and to other sponsors in Riverside County.) The Volags' inability to recruit sponsors may explain the number of sponsors who turned the Cuban refugees out. Because of the scarcity of volunteers, Volag representatives could not afford to discriminate inappropriate sponsors from others.

While the Indochinese refugees were most often seen as innocent victims, the Cubans were rarely seen as such. They were successfully stigmatized by Castro, by the media, and by the acts of a few of them, as "scum," rioters, criminals, homosexuals, mentally ill people, and problematic workers. Their motives for flight were suspect; many by self-report sought economic self-improvement and a freer supply of consumer goods rather than freedom of speech or freedom from fear of persecution.

To this point, I have compared public response to the Cubans and the Indochinese refugees, considering the former an instance where popular perception rejected casting of the Cubans as innocent victims, causing congregations to refuse to sponsor them despite the classification of them as political refugees and (belatedly) welcome by President Carter. Yet, United States recognition of the plight of refugees may lag behind that of congregational refugee advocates. During the period in which the Cubans were admitted, the U.S. State Department and Immigration and Naturalization Service refused to recognize the Haitians who arrived (like the Cubans) in small boats on American shores without papers as political refugees, despite evidence from human rights observers and Amnesty International that such people were fleeing from well-founded fear of persecution and might risk their lives if returned. Congregational Volags assisted the Haitians (jailed when caught) to petition the courts in 1979–80, and a federal court ordered the government to halt deportations of the Haitians without due process. Subsequently, the Reagan administration arrested the influx by interdicting boats with Haitians at sea, alleging that the government was conducting inquiries as to whether they fit the definition of political refugees on the water—without observers and lawyers.

Some religious groups and congregations also began giving sanctuary and established an "underground railway" across the United States in the 1980s for Salvadoran and Guatemalan refugees fleeing from massacres and civil war who were not categorically recognized as political refugees by the U.S. State Department as Cuban and eastern European refugees were. Their individual requests for asylum were usually denied. These Central Americans were decreed to be illegal aliens and thus might be pressed (if caught) to agree to their "voluntary return" or be prosecuted in the United States. Their helpers justify their civil disobedience and violation of U.S. law in terms of obedience to a higher law and the duty to resist oppression and injustice.[29] Thus, one sees a pattern among these helpers similar to that among helpers of Jews during the Holocaust described in chapter 2: the victims are conceived of as innocent, and defined within an all-encompassing universe of obligation; a higher law legitimates disobedience to secular authority; the duty to resist is justified by leaders in terms of the values and traditions of the group, and the action is socially organized along a network of preexisting associations that are reinforced (in this case) by formal organizations with staff, resources, and regular communication channels.

One may also infer that the United States' support of the governments of Haiti and El Salvador biases the State Department against labeling people fleeing from these nations as political refugees, as it has labeled emigrés categorically as refugees. Thus, the initial categorical recognition or denial that cohorts of aliens are political refugees is still an indirect product of U.S. foreign policy despite the passage of the 1980 Refugee Act setting down a universalistic definition of political refugees.

Some Recommendations for Public Policy

Both for the sake of law and of justice, the first responsibility of the United States government should be to administer U.S. law—which incorporates the UN definition of political refugees—without bias based on the type of regime from which people flee or based on their relationship with American ethnic groups. Bias in official recognition of refugees may reinforce public disinterest and cynicism toward all refugees.

When refugees are admitted, planners must ask: where and how should they be settled? Rather than aim (as in 1975) for an unattainable policy of equal dispersion that denies refugees the collective right to community, government policies focusing on cluster settlement (as recommended by the Select Commision on Immigration and Refugee Policy) could provide refugees and communities the advantages of group or congregational sponsorship and ethnic communities.[30] Such a policy could attempt to maximize the benefits of ethnic community and seek to avoid intergroup conflicts associated with high concentrations by encouraging selected communities and regions that are desirable sites of resettlement to accept specified numbers of refugees, leading to modest concentrations of refugees of one ethnic group. Some critieria for target communities, counties, or regions might include: the economic capacity of the area (indexed by the percent unemployed and unfulfilled demand for labor in local industries) and the match between the skills of the refugees and economic needs; the presence of a related ethnic group (a desirable criterion but not a prerequisite), and the potential for integration or ethnic conflict (related to the percent and status of other minorities with whom the newcomers may be in competition); the costs of resettlement (related to the price and supply of housing and public transportation and the cost of living); the similarity of climate; and not least important, the social infrastructure of churches, voluntary organization, and other institutions that can mobilize sponsors and helpers. There is already some evidence that planned regional or state resettlement has led to more integration and less dependency and helped ethnic communities to reestablish themselves.[31]

Federal policy also needs to be examined as to how it itself impacts upon secondary migration. While the refugees' rights to move as freely as do American citizens must be respected and sponsors must be prepared to anticipate saying goodbye, an area of refugee resettlement that becomes a staging point or way-station is less likely to become a community as the outflow instigates refugees staying behind to leave. Further, McInnis points out that disappointed sponsors can transmit negative attitudes toward other potential sponsors.[32] A uniform policy of benefits for refugees and a more flexible criterion for placement of resources in sponsoring communities might encourage more refugees to stay. Both "entitlements" and expectations of refugees affect sponsors, Volags, and federal costs and impact on refugees' mobility. Refugees in states with fewer benefits compare themselves invidiously to others from the same town or camp in states with better benefits and naturally feel deprived. Whereas this has perhaps only accounted for a few moves from Riverside County, representatives of the Volags with whom I talked report that Indochinese refugees now arrive here with a sense of entitlement based upon rumors of welfare and schooling freely available in some states, as Palmieri noted. The comparisons among refugees of the disparity of benefits and criticisms of same have been remarked on by refugees in the United States and Canada.[33] It seems implausible to believe that explanation of the federal-state system will undo this sense of relative deprivation if they are consigned to a sponsor in a less-favored state. Given the fact that refugees qualify for food stamps, Medicaid, and public assistance on the same criteria as do citizens without employment or resources, it is impossible to foresee how this recommendation could be carried out unless a national income policy and health maintenance program replaced the diverse federal and state welfare programs in the United States. A national policy that secured minimal health, nutritional, and housing needs as entitlements might also remove the disincentives for the working poor—and new refugees—to get jobs.

As Palmieri observed, voluntary donations and voluntarism is unlikely to become a substitute for national commitment and planning, but federal policy might spur voluntary commitment.[34] Federal policy might materially ease the most troubling task of sponsors lacking ESL programs for refugees in scattered communities by assigning federally funded master teachers to work with sponsors and school volunteers to tutor adult refugees and their children. Present criteria for funding services often deny refugees in small towns such services, giving the refugees further incentive to move. School systems without a minimum number of Indochinese children find that they cannot offer ESL classes, and teachers often have no time for one-to-one work with non–English-speaking students or no background, if they have time and goodwill. Complementary and more flexible working relationships with government and federally funded "service providers"—especially master teachers and job developers—and community planning may actually encourage more sponsorship.

As accepting refugees becomes recognized as a national obligation, the level and use of resources for resettlement must be assessed to assure equity of entitlements among refugees and motivate them to become self-supporting as soon as possible for their own sake and for the sake of future refugees seeking admission. To be politically and ethnically defensible, entitlements for refugees must be comparable to entitlements for citizens with similar disadvantages—the homeless, the jobless, and the non–English speakers.

At the time of writing (Winter 1983), the estimates of the homeless (perhaps half a million across the United States) and jobless (over 10 percent of the labor force) confirm that the United States is in a depression. Those who in the past have been sensitized to helping the needy stranger are confronted not only with refugees but their neighbors as victims. The president of the United States has asked private philanthropies to compensate for government cutbacks. In New York City the mayor demands churches and synagogues take in the homeless. A surfeit of victims could lead to a denial of individual and public responsibility or a new collective demand that government become responsible for all its citizens. It is more likely, in such a case, that public leadership would draw out voluntary commitment than that voluntary commitment can substitute for public commitment.

Rather than voluntary initiative being a substitute for government response, governmental response in the United States spurred congregational responses during the Indochinese refugee crisis. Responsibility for the refugees was accepted by sponsors as a joint responsibility, producing benefits for refugees, sponsors, local communities, and the nation. Not only should we consider in future planning the impact sponsors have on refugees but the impact of refugees on sponsors and sponsors on the community. Sponsorship met a need for congregational sponsors similar to the need that Titmuss recognized among blood donors:

> . . . as individuals they were, it may be said, taking part in the creation of a greater good transcending the good of self-love. To love themselves they recognized the need to "love" the stranger.[35]

Titmuss goes on to recommend that:

> . . . the notion of social rights—a product of the twentieth century—should thus embrace the "Right to Give" in non-material as well as material ways.[36]

Refugee sponsorship offers a unique way to exercise that right, a right as often constrained by routinized charity and professional service providers who regard the public role as solely that of check-writers as it is by profit-making organizations. It also enabled many citizens to directly participate in resettlement as members of congregations. Within the congregations, it was the initiative of the enthusiasts who gathered support in their congregations and magnified support throughout the community, which drew more Americans to affirm that, as Arthur Brown put it:

These are our people.

Appendix
Sponsor Questionnaire

1. Name
2. Address and Phone No.
3. Sex
4. Race
5. Age
6. Marital Status
7. Children (list age/sex of each)
8. a) Occupation
   b) Employer
   c) (If not in labor market) occupation of principal wage earner in family
   d) employer of above
9. Education
10. Size of town
11. Length of residence at present address
12. Length of residence in county
13. Length of residence in state
14. Birthplace
    Outside US   Cont.
    In US (specify NY, other NE, region other than NE)
15. Birthplace of father
                   mother
16. Languages spoken in parents' home
17. Languages spoken in own home
18. Year arrived in US

19. Veteran status and military service
20. Sponsoring Church/Group
    role in above
    role in RIC
    role in church
    name of church
21. How long have you been a member of *X* church?
    How long have you been a (Presbyterian, Catholic, etc.)?
22. Are you an active member? (Probe participation, activities, Board/council membership)
23. Have you participated in any other Christian movements (apart from your church) and/or interfaith movements in the last four years? (Name/type of movement/organization)
24. How many people in your church do you know well/as friends/on a visiting basis?
25. Would you say that most of your friends, some of your friends, or few of your friends belong to the same church?
26. People express many different ideas about what it means to be a Christian, to be a good Christian. What is your idea?
27. Can you think of any people—parents, teachers, public figures, others—who have influenced your willingness to stand up for your beliefs and act on them?
28. Do you belong to any civic or other groups/organizations outside of the church and religious organizations? (For each, probe extent of recent participation—office holding, donating money/time, voting, attendance: probe civic, service, PTA's, fraternal, labor, professional)
29. Would you label yourself politically conservative, middle-of-the-road, liberal, or in some other way?
30. What was the last election in which you voted?
31. Have you ever campaigned for a candidate for office? When? What office?
    Have you ever written to one of your representatives? (Probe when, which office-holder(s), which issues and how often.)
32. Do you feel strongly about any current public issues? Which ones?
33. During the period of the U.S. involvement in the war in Indochina, did you have strong feelings one way or the other about our role there? Did they change between 1963 and 1975? Did you act on them in any way? Have your opinions changed since that time?
34. When did you first *consider* getting involved in the sponsorship of Indochinese refugees?
35. What drew your attention to this (them)? (Probe role of others—public leaders, minister, other sponsors, appeal of previous refugees—media, etc.)

36. Had you known any Asian people before? From what nation? How did you know them? Did you discuss it with them?

37. Had your church ever sponsored refugees before? (If yes) Were you involved in the sponsorship? What did you think of that experience? (If no) What did they (people who had been involved/others) say about the experience?

38. Had you ever been a member of a church or other group which had sponsored refugees? (Probe/same as above)

39. Had you known any people around here who had sponsored? Did you talk with them about it? (Probe response)

40. What kinds of doubts or worries (fears?) did you have when you first thought about sponsorship? What did you do next?

41. At what point was the idea of sponsorship brought up in your church/group?

42. How did this occur? Who brought it up?

43. How was commitment to sponsor made? By whom? (Probe authorization)

44. If sponsorship accepted: Did you consider sponsorship as a single congregation, two congregations, or as a community?

45. (If more than one considered): What made you choose as you did?

46. How did your committee get started?

47. How many people were first involved?

48. Did you know them before this? How and how well did you know them?

49. How did the number involved grow? (Probe characteristics of people attracted, previous acquaintance, activity in church, etc.)

50. What part did your minister play?

51. Once the commitment was made, how were officers and/or committee chairs chosen?

52. How was the committee organized?

53. What were the first tasks or problems the committee set out to do/resolve before applying for sponsorship? How did it go about that?

54. What resources did the committee gather? (Probe sources/amounts money, furnishing, clothing, housing [if relevant] gathered in advance.)

55. How many contributed toward putting these (resources) together? How many of these were people who had before expressed sympathy for sponsorship, had expressed opposition or negative feelings, or had not expressed anything before?

56. When and how did you choose to sponsor through the Volag you chose?

57. Had you requested a specific refugee family when you applied to them?

58a. (If yes to 57.) How did you become aware of this family?

58b. If related to other refugees in region, indicate to whom they were related and relationship.

59. (If no to 57.) What did you tell them about what kind/numbers of refugees you were willing to accept?

60. When did they refer one or more refugee family (household) to you for acceptance?

61. Who was that? Record family surname, sex/age/relationship of members and nation of origin/ethnic group.

62. (If more than one family referred [60.]): How did you choose among them?

63a. How long did you wait before they arrived?

63b. When did they arrive?

64. What other contact did you have with this agency?

65. Would you say the agency was helpful or could have been more helpful?

66. (If response negative to 65.): In what way were you dissatisfied?

67. Did you draw upon the grant per capita promised by the agency? Did you have any delay/trouble in getting it?

68. After refugees arrived, where did they live? (If in temporary housing or with member): How long were they there? Had you planned on this?

69a. (If living with member for more than two weeks): What kinds of problems did they face living together?

69b. What kinds of problems did they encounter breaking up?

70. How did your group take care of their needs once they were settled?
    Probe

medical	housekeeping skills
social service/social security reg.	driving—trans. arrange.
school placement & ESL training	(teaching driving)
employment	babysitting

71. What part did you play?

72. How many hours a week would you estimate you were involved during the first week/month they were here? After that?

73. How did you feel about that?

74. Was one member of your group more responsible for attending to their needs than others? Who was this? (name/role)

75. How did this come about?

76. How did this work out?

77. Was one member more involved as a friend or guide to them than others? Who was this? (name/role)

78. How did this come about?

79. How did this work out?

80. How did you and others communicate with the family sponsored?

(Probe direct verbal, nonverbal communication, modeling, doing things together, expressions of affect: use of translators, dictionaries, intermediaries—probe role of latter: using/rejecting use of English after training)

81. How did your committee go about making decisions/resolving problems that came up? (Probe methods—meetings, calls—formal and informal networks, specific/diffuse roles, withdrawal/assumption of roles, expansion/diminishing of commitment.)

82. What kinds of questions/problems came up in your relationship with the family that you had not anticipated? How did you deal with them?

83. What kinds of problems/issues came up that you had anticipated? How did you deal with them?

84. How did the actual experience change relationships within your group?

85. How did the family relate to your church/group?

86. Did you try to involve them in some way? (Probe explanations of sponsorship involved, nature of church/committee.)

87. (If church attendance mentioned): Were they asked to come? Did someone pick them up to take them? How often did they come?

88. (If response was they came voluntarily): Why do you think they came?

89. How did members of congregation react to them?

90. When did the family become financially independent?

91. Did your relationship to them change at that time or sometime after that? How did it change?

If family has left or is considering leaving the region:

92. When (how long after arrival) did they start thinking about it? (Probe source of knowledge.)

93. Did they tell you or some other member of the committee about it?

94. How did you react to this?

95. When did they make the decision to go?

96. How was this communicated to you?

97. How did you and members of your committee feel about their decision?

98. What did you do when you knew they were leaving?

99. How and where did they go?

100. How did they leave? (Probe committee role/response to departure preparations.)

101. How did you and other members feel at this time?

102. Have you heard from them since? (Probe frequency/nature/form of communications from whom.)

103. If first sponsorship is ended: Has your committee considered sponsoring another family?

If decision made:
104. What factors affected their decision?
105. How do you feel now about the whole experience?
106. Has it changed you in any way?
107. Has it changed your expectations about people?

Notes

Preface

1. "Poll Finds U.S. Public Favors Responsible, Responsive Refugee Admissions," *Refugee Reports*, 15 June 1984, 1–13.

2. Testimony presented in evidence before the House Post Office and Civil Service Committee on 27 June 1985 is summarized in "Statistical Evidence Indicates Many Salvadorans in U.S. Flee from Violence," *Refugee Reports*, 16 August 1985, 1.

Chapter 1. Collective Altruism, Helping, and Lifesaving Behavior

1. C. T. Onions, ed., *Oxford Universal Dictionary on Historical Principles* (Oxford: Clarendon Press, 1955), 51.

2. Gerhard Lenski and Jean Lenski, *Human Societies: An Introduction to Macrosociology* (New York: McGraw Hill, 1974), 148–49.

3. Jeremy A. Silver, *A History of Judaism*, vol. 1, *From Abraham to Maimonides* (New York: Basic Books, 1963), 175.

4. Because the radical Protestant reformers defined all Christians as brothers in Christ, they concluded none should charge interest or benefit from their brothers' debt and they called for the abolition of the interest (labeled usury), which bore so heavily upon the peasants. Ultimately, their demand and definition of usury was defeated in the context of ideologies and interests. Protestant theologians such as Luther (who initially waffled on this point) and Calvin finally rejected the proposed standard and discriminated between usury (excessive interest), still forbidden, and interest, which was decreed tolerable. Nelson views their role in creating "rationales of conscience" as critical in the making of the modern mind, which legitimated the new norms of capitalism. These justified the morality of self-interest and the accumulation (and loan) of capital. See Benjamin Nelson, *The Idea of Usury: From Tribal Brotherhood to Universal Otherhood,* 2nd ed. (Chicago: University of Chicago Press, 1969), 229–30.

5. Frederick A. Norwood, *Strangers and Exiles: A History of Religious Refugees,* vol. 1 (Nashville: Abingdon press, 1969), 105–11, 116–23.

6. U.S. Committee for Refugees, *1980 World Refugee Survey* (New York: U.S. Committee for Refugees, 1981), 33.

7. John A. Rawls, *A Theory of Justice* (Cambridge, Mass.: Belknap Press, 1971).

8. Garrett J. Hardin, *The Limits of Altruism: An Ecologist's View of Survival* (Bloomington: Indiana University Press, 1977).

9. Cecil Woodham-Smith, *The Great Hunger, Ireland, 1845–1849* (New York: Harper and Row, 1962), 410–11.

10. See M. Olson, Jr., *The Logic of Collective Action* (Cambridge: Harvard University Press, 1965); and Jane A. Piliavin et al., *Emergency Intervention* (New York: Academic Press, 1981).

11. Robert A. Nisbet, *The Sociological Tradition* (New York: Basic Books, 1966), 71–82.

12. Emile Durkheim, *Suicide: A Study in Sociology,* trans. J. A. Spaulding and George SImpson (New York: Free Press, 1951; first pub. 1897).

13. Three of the four types of social action discriminated by Max Weber (omitting *zweckrational*) are compatible with altruism. One may also relate Parsons's discrimination of universalistic versus particularistic norms and values to orientations toward helping others outside one's membership collectivity. See Talcott Parsons et al., eds., *Theories of Society: Foundation of Modern Sociological Theory,* vol. 1 (New York: Free Press, 1961), 43–44. Theodorson and Theodorson relate altruism to Parsons's dichotomy between self and collectivity orientation in T. Parsons and E. A. Shils, eds., *Toward a General Theory of Action* (1951) in their *A Modern Dictionary of Sociology* (New York: Thomas Y. Crowell Co., 1969), 375–76.

14. Peter M. Blau, *Exchange and Power in Social Life* (New York: Wiley, 1964).

15. Richard Dawkins, *The Selfish Gene* (New York: Oxford University Press, 1976).

16. J. B. Schneewind, "Sociobiology, Social Policy, and Nirvana," in *Sociobiology and Human Nature,* ed. Michael S. Gregory, Anita Silver, and Diane Such (San Francisco: Jossey-Bass, 1978), 235.

17. Edward O. Wilson, *On Human Nature* (Cambridge: Harvard University Press, 1978), 157.

18. Alvin Gouldner, "The Norm of Reciprocity: A Preliminary Statement," *American Sociological Review* 15, no. 3 (April 1960): 161–78.

19. Lenski and Lenski, *Human Societies,* 149.

20. David Collard, *Altruism and Economics: A Study of Non-Selfish Economics* (New York: Oxford University press, 1978).

21. Richard M. Titmuss, *The Gift Relationship: From Human Blood to Social Policy* (New York: Pantheon Books, 1971).

22. Collard, *Altruism and Economics,* 156.

23. Gouldner, "The Norm of Reciprocity," 161–78.

24. Richard Hofstasdter, *Social Darwinism in American Thought* (New York: George Braziller, 1955).

25. Stephen L. Chorover, *From Genesis to Genocide: The Meaning of Human Nature and the Power of Behavior Control* (Cambridge: MIT Press, 1979), 29, 97; see also Stephen J. Gould, *The Mismeasure of Man* (New York: Norton, 1981).

26. Harry Elmer Barnes, "The Social and Political Philosophy of August Comte: Positivist Utopia and the Religion of Humanity," in *An Introduction to the History of Sociology,* ed. Harry Elmer Barnes (Chicago: University of Chicago Press, 1948), 93.

27. Peter Kropotkin, *Mutual Aid: A Factor of Evolution* (1890–96; reprint, Boston: Extending Horizons, 1955).

28. Ervin Staub, *Positive Social Behavior and Morality,* 2 vols. (New York: Academic Press, 1979).

29. Ibid., 2: 12.

30. Lauren Wispé, ed., *Altruism, Sympathy and Helping* (New York: Academic Press, 1978).

31. Piliavin et al., *Emergency Intervention,* chaps. 1, 10.

32. Ibid., 4.

33. Ibid., 199.

34. Ibid., 196.

35. Ibid., 240–43, 250.

36. Lester Ward, *Dynamic Sociology,* vol. 1 (New York: Appleton, 1883), 369.

37. Robert K. Merton, *Social Theory and Social Structure,* rev. ed. (Glencoe, Ill.: The Free Pree of Glencoe, 1957), 365.

38. Jacqueline R. Macauley and Leonard Berkowitz, "Overview," in *Altruism and Helping Behavior: Social Psychological Studies of Some Antecedents and Consequences,* ed. J. Macauley and L. Berkowitz (New York: Academic Press, 1970), 2.

39. Justin Aronfreed, "The Socialization of Altruistic and Sympathetic Behavior: Some Theoretical and Experimental Analyses," in Macauley and Berkowitz, eds., *Altruism and Helping Behavior,* 105.

40. Pitirim A. Sorokin, *Altruistic Love: A Study of American "Good Neighbors" and Christian Saints* (1950; reprint, New York: Kraus Reprint Co., 1969).

41. Ibid., 57.

42. Ibid., 52.

43. David Rosenham, "The Natural Socialization of Altruistic Autonomy," in Macauley and Berkowitz, eds., *Altruism and Helping Behavior,* 251–69.

44. Ibid., 252.

45. Perry London, "The Rescuers: Motivational Hypotheses about Christians Who Saved Jews from the Nazis," in Macauley and Berkowitz, eds., *Altruism and Helping Behavior,* 241–50.

46. Ibid., 242.

47. Ibid., 248.

48. Eva Fogelman and Valerie Weiner, "The Few, the Brave, and the Noble," *Psychology Today,* August 1985, 61–64.

49. Frances Grossman, "A Psychological Study of Gentiles Who Saved the Lives of Jews during the Holocaust," in *Toward the Understanding and Prevention of Genocide: Proceedings of the International Conference on the Holocaust and Genocide,* ed. Israel W. Charney (Boulder, Colo.: Westview Press, 1984), 202–16.

50. Nechama Tec, *When Light Pierced the Darkness: Christian Rescue of Jews in Nazi-Occupied Poland* (New York: Oxford University Press, 1986), 188.

51. Fernand Leboucher, *Incredible Mission,* trans. J. F. Bernard (Garden City, N.Y.: Doubleday, 1969).

52. Helen Fein, *Accounting for Genocide: National Responses and Jewish Victimization during the Holocaust* (New York: Free Press, 1979), 50–120, 143–164.

Chapter 2. Collective Altruism, Refugee and Rescue Policy

1. Malcolm J. Proudfoot, *European Refugees, 1939–1952: A Study in Forced Population Movement* (Evanston, Ill.: Northwestern University Press, 1956), 291, 341, 371–80.

2. Alistair Horne, *A Savage War of Peace: Algeria 1954–1962* (New York: Viking Press, 1977), 533; Leo Kuper, *Genocide: Its Political Use in the Twentieth Century* (New Haven: Yale University Press, 1981), 69.

3. The concept of "middleman minority" is that of Hubert Blalock, Jr.; see *Towards a Theory of Minority-Group Relations* (New York: Cparicon, 1970). For studies of persecution

of "alien pariahs," see James H. Mittelman and Oukar S. Marwah, *Asian Alien Pariahs: A Cross-Regional Perspective* (Denver: University of Denver Studies in Race and Nations Center of International Race Relations, 1975).

4. United Nations, *Human Rights: A Compilation of International Instruments of the United Nations* (New York: U.N., 1973), 72.

5. Michael Harrington, *Towards a Democratic Left: A Radical Program for a New Majority* (New York: Macmillan, 1968), 291.

6. Fein, *Accounting for Genocide,* chaps. 3, 4, 6, 7; Yad Vashem, *Rescue Attempts during the Holocaust: Proceedings of the Second Yad Vashem International Historical Conference, Jerusalem, April 8–11, 1974* (Jerusalem: Yad Vashem, 1977).

7. Hannah Arendt, *The Origins of Totalitarianism,* rev. ed. (New York: Harcourt, Brace and World, 1966), 295–96.

8. Henry Feingold, *The Politics of Rescue: The Roosevelt Administration and the Holocaust, 1938–1945* (New Brunswick, N.J.: Rutgers University Press, 1970), 303.

9. Bernard Wasserstein,. *Britain and the Jews of Europe 1939–1945* (Oxford: Clarendon Press, 1979), 207.

10. On the U.S. State Department (especially the role of Breckenridge Long), see Feingold, *The Politics of Rescue;* Arthur D. Morse, *While Six Million Died: A Chronicle of American Apathy* (New York: Random House, 1968); and David S. Wyman, *The Abandonment of the Jews: America and the Holocaust 1941–1945* (New York: Pantheon Books, 1984). On the British Foreign Office, see Wasserstein, *Britain and the Jews of Europe;* and Martin Gilbert, *Auschwitz and the Allies* (New York: Holt, Rinehart and Winston, 1981).

11. Charles Herbert Stember et al., *Jews in the Mind of America* (New York: Basic Books, 1966), 137–38.

12. Fein, *Accounting for Genocide,* 167.

13. Feingold, *The Politics of Rescue,* 21–32; Saul S. Friedman, *No Haven for the Oppressed: United States Policy Toward Jewish Refugees, 1938–1945* (Detroit: Wayne State University Press, 1973), 61–63.

14. Proudfoot, *European Refugees,* 319.

15. Fein, *Accounting for Genocide,* 175–82.

16. Seymour M. Finger, ed., *American Jewry during the Holocaust* (New York: American Jewish Commission on the Holocaust, March 1984), Appendix 3, 7–8.

17. Wyman, *The Abandonment of the Jews,* 328–29.

18. David S. Wyman, *Paper Walls: America and the Refugee Crisis, 1938–1941* (Amherst: University of Massachusetts Press, 1968), 23–26, 68–71.

19. Haim Genizi, "American Interfaith Cooperation on Behalf of Refugees from Nazism, 1933–1945," *American Jewish History* 70, no. 3 (March 1981): 347–61.

20. George Gallup, *The Gallup Poll 1935–1971,* vol. 1 (New York: Random House, 1971), 229–30, 236–37.

21. Robert W. Ross, *So It Was True: The American Protestant Press and the Nazi Persecution of the Jews, 1933–1945* (Minneapolis: University of Minnesota Press, 1980), 104, 135, 270.

22. Wyman, *The Abandonment of the Jews,* 317.

23. Ibid., 157–77, 200–202.

24. Fein, *Accounting for Genocide,* 171–73.

25. Gilbert, *Auschwitz and the Allies,* 271–72, 284, 300–320; Fein, *Accounting for Genocide,* 173.

26. Fein, *Accounting for Genocide,* 33.

27. Ibid., 35–36.

28. Leni Yahil, *The Rescue of Danish Jewry: Test of a Democracy,* trans. Morris Gradel (Philadelphia: Jewish Publication Society of America, 1969), 41–44.

29. Fein, *Accounting for Genocide,* 149.

30. Philip Hallie, *Lest Innocent Blood Be Shed: The Story of the Village of Le Chambon and How Goodness Happened There* (New York: Harper and Row, 1979).

31. Ibid., 286.

32. Tatiana Berenstein and Adam Rutkowski, *Assistance to the Jews in Poland,* trans. Edward Rothert (Warsaw: Polinia, 1963), 45; Penina Schlossberg, "The Story of Naliboki," *Yalkut Moreshut* 2 (December 1964).

33. Fein, *Accounting for Genocide,* 47.

34. Vietnam, pressed by war with China and Kampuchea and by a declining economy, solved several problems at the same time by forcing its citizens of ethnic Chinese origin (from whom the trading class were predominantly drawn before 1975) to flee. Their gold, extracted through a confiscatory exit tax and bribes, was useful to the government as foreign exchange, helping to repay Vietnam's debt to the U.S.S.R.; the population that had to be fed was diminished; and last, a category of citizens who might be accused of dual loyalty (to China and Vietnam) was expelled. See the *New York Times,* 12 June 1979, 1 and 3 August 1979, 1, regarding motives.

35. Barry Wain, *The Refused: The Agony of the Indochina Refugees* (New York: Simon and Schuster, 1981), 196–205.

36. Ibid., 156.

37. Gordon Thomas, *Voyage of the Damned* (New York: Stein and Day, 1974).

38. Fein, *Accounting for Genocide,* 183.

39. Wain, *The Refused,* 133.

40. *New York Times,* 25 June 1980, 3.

41. Alfred A. Haesler, *The Lifeboat is Full: Switzerland and the Refugees, 1933–1945,* trans. Charles Lamm Markham (New York: Funk and Wagnalls, 1969), 326.

42. The *New York Times Index* enables one to make an approximate comparison of the space focused on a series of events by measuring the number of inches of columns used to abstract and index the stories of such events. While the Index for 1979 had 165 inches of column space focused on Vietnamese refugees and expatriates, in 1939 the Index had 241 inches on the persecution of the Jews in Germany and Central Europe and the Jewish refugees. Over twice as much summary column space was filled with news on the persecution of the Jews in Germany in 1938 (the year of the state-organized pogrom known as Kristallnacht and internment of 20,000 Jewish men in concentration camps) as was taken by the Vietnamese refugees in the Index of 1978 (136 inches versus 57 inches). Whereas the news of Jewish refugees in 1938 was indexed under "Jews, Germany" for 1939, it was indexed under "Minorities and Oppressed Groups," indicating the broadening and increased abstraction of the problem, denying the identity of the victim.

More news stories in 1979 focused on Cambodia than on Vietnamese refugees, especially on the war between Cambodia and Vietnam and the subsequent famine in Cambodia, which drew worldwide attention and activated international relief efforts. It is possible that the Southeast Asian refugees were more visible in 1979 because of the reiterated image of the starving Cambodians, which reinforced the image of the refugees impressed on a general public, which did not discriminate the source of victimization of the faces on their television screens.

43. John Donne, quoted in Helen C. White et al., *Seventeenth Century Verse and Prose,* vol. 1 (New York: Macmillan, 1951).

44. George Gallup, *The Gallup Poll 1972–1977,* vol. 1 (Wilmington, Del.: Scholarly Resources, 1980).

45. George Gallup, *Public Opinion 1979* (Wilmington, Del.: Scholarly Resources, 1980), 246–48.

46. *New York Times,* 15 July 1979, 16.

47. By contrast, in Canada the sponsorship movement was a multilevel citizens' movement with many secular and ad-hoc groups forming in order to press the government to fullfil its pledge to match federally subsidized sponsorships with private sponsorships. However, in the United States, the sponsorship movement itself was generated by the denominationally affiliated and other voluntary agencies contracting with the State Department to resettle refugees, and these agencies did not instigate new group formation.

48. Indochinese refugees were most likely to be drawn from the groups who were fighting against the insurgency—the people whom the United States was alleged to be fighting to save. Refugees granted parole status by the attorney-general are ranked in four preferential categories. First rank (preference) is granted to those with immediate family in the United States, those who have worked for the U.S. government directly, and those who are at risk because of their indirect association with the United States, such as police and intelligence agents of the former pro-western regimes of Indochina.

Chapter 3. Becoming Sponsors

1. Barney G. Glaser and Anselm L. Strauss, *The Discovery of Grounded Theory: Strategies for Qualitative Research* (Chicago: Aldine, 1967).

2. Ervin Staub, *Positive Social Behavior and Morality*, vol. 1 (New York: Academic Press, 1979), 151.

3. Ibid., 161–62.

4. John D. McCarthy and Mayer N. Zald, "Resource Mobilization and Social Movements: A Partial Theory," *American Journal of Sociology* 82, no. 6 (December 1976): 1212–42.

5. Two of the sponsoring congregations in Riverside County were excluded from the number from which the sample was picked because of the goals of the study. In one case, the refugee household that the committee had "assured" (agreed to accept) had not arrived at the time the study began and the study was restricted to sponsors who had had an opportunity to resettle refugees in order to provide data for the second focus of the study (see chapter 3). The other case excluded was a church made up exclusively of members of a related Asian ethnic group that I excluded in order to maintain the focus of the study on the interaction of refugees with sponsors of predominantly native-born parentage who are English-speaking and usually lack the ability to communicate in the refugees' own language(s).

6. This occurred after the committee had spent almost half their budget on rental of an apartment for three months due to the bad advice of a Volag representative who told them that the family they had agreed to support was to arrive imminently. After problems impeded their processing, another family was assigned to the sponsors and their processing was delayed. The committee disbanded because the largest church on the committee—the church that had instigated the interfaith sponsorship—voted to withdraw as a sponsor, fearing their limited resources might lead the refugees to reliance on public assistance and subsidies they wished to avoid. Their fears were aggravated by the apprehension of opposition within the church to refugees, minorities, and welfare and their reluctance to confirm the justifications against sponsorship advanced by the opponents.

7. All population statistics for 1980 are based on U.S. census figures supplied by the Riverside County Department of Planning. Census figures for 1970 and earlier are taken from the Riverside County Department of Planning *Data Book* (1974).

8. Unemployment figures are based on the monthly Department of Labor Reports of the state in which Riverside County is located.

9. The ethnic and black churches may either be less inclined to consider sponsorship of Indochinese refugees because of particular commitments to their constituency that comes

first (limiting the resources available) and/or preferences for other refugees from similar backgrounds. In a few cases, members of these churches questioned about whether their congregation had or would consider sponsorship expressed their opinion that their membership, composed of older, non–English-speaking, first-generation immigrants, would not be good cultural guides and/or would not feel competent as sponsors; it was not that they lacked sympathy for refugees and new immigrants but they they were themselves unassimilated immigrants. A Chinese ethnic congregation did sponsor Chinese-Vietnamese refugees, and a secular Hispanic community association sponsored Cuban refugees; both groups were led by educated professionals similar to other sponsors surveyed.

10. Rodney Stark et al., "Ministers as Moral Guides: The Sounds of Silence," in *Religion in Sociological Perspective: Essays in the Empirical Study of Religion,* ed. Charles Y. Glock (Belmont, Calif.: Wadsworth Pub. Co., 1973), 163–86.

11. C. Kirk Hadaway, "Changing Brands: Denominational Switching and Membership Change," in *Yearbook of American and Canadian Churches 1980,* ed. Constant Jacquet, Jr. (Nashville: Abington Press, 1980), 265.

12. This discrimination of Fichter between the church as an association and a community is elaborated by Charles Y. Glock, Benjamin B. Ringer, and Earl R. Babbie, *To Comfort and to Challenge* (Berkeley: University of California Press, 1967).

13. Sorokin, *Altruistic Love;* London, "The Rescuers"; Rosenham, "Natural Socialization of Altruistic Behavior."

14. Sidney Verba, Norman H. Nie, and Jae-On Kim, *Participation and Political Equality: A Seven-Nation Comparison* (New York: Cambridge University Press, 1978), 176.

15. Raymond Wolfinger and J. Rosenstohn, *Who Votes* (New Haven: Yale University Press, 1980), 17, 23.

16. John D. Holm and John P. Robinson, "Ideology and the American Voter," *Public Opinion Quarterly* 42, no. 2 (Summer 1978): 238.

17. The one question most regularly asked between 1963 and 1975 by Gallup was whether the respondent considered that involvement in Vietnam had been a mistake. The percent answering yes increased from 21 percent in 1965 to 61 percent in 1970 and did not alter materially after that, while the percent saying no dropped from 64 percent in 1965 to 28 percent in 1971 and did not change substantively thereafter. See George Gallup, *The Gallup Poll 1972–1977,* vol. 1, *1972–1975* (Wilmington, Del.: Scholarly Resources, Inc., 1978), 87–89; *The Gallup Poll 1935–1971,* vol. 3, *1959–1971* (New York: Random House, 1972), 1971, 2031, 2086, 2125, 2254, 2309.

18. Ira Gallobin, "Hospitality and Hostility: Two U.S. Policies on Immigration," mimeographed paper submitted to Consultation on Overstayed and Undocumented Persons Sponsored by the National Council of Churches, 5 May 1978.

19. The survey of studies on this question by the Interagency Task Force on Immigration Policy *Staff Report* (Washington, D.C.: Departments of Justice, Labor, and State, March 1979), chap. 6, relate the short- and long-term impact of immigration to the development of the economy, the structure of the labor market, the point of the economic cycle in which immigrants enter, the number of immigrants, their age and occupational distribution, the services they require presently, and their potential contribution in taxes and productivity as well as their concentration.

20. L. Festinger, *A Theory of Cognitive Dissonance* Evangston, Ill.: Row, Peterson, 1957).

Chapter 4. The Achievement of Group Sponsorship

1. Howard Adelman, "Understanding Backlash," in *The Indochinese Refugee Movement: The Canadian Experience,* ed. Howard Adelman (Toronto: Operation Lifelife, 1980), 23–27.

2. Ibid., 104–6.

3. Penny Van Esterik, "In-Home Sponsorship for Southeast Asian Refugees," *Journal of Refugee Resettlement* 1, no. 2 (March 1981): 18–26.

4. Instances of bitterness and mourning among sponsors of refugees who have left that I have heard about secondhand are often also cases where the sponsors blame the refugees for leaving; by contrast, none of the sponsors in the cases later discussed in the chapter blamed the refugees, however much they regretted their departure. Furthermore, other sponsorship developers and coordinators consistently talk about this as a problem with congregational sponsors. Judith May, discussing "The Vermont Experience," says, "The hardest part of my job has been to deal with the anguish of sponsors when the family decides to leave. The departure usually happens almost overnight and without warning. I now talk with sponsors about this as part of their orientation." See *Journal of Refugee Resettlement* 1, no. 3 (May 1981): 31–35.

5. Most Indochinese peoples (and refugees) are slight and thin compared to North Americans, so they visibly confirm the sponsors' expectation and usually evoked a visceral sensation that they needed protection. A Vietnamese refugee who was tall and robustly built evoked surprise. Added to this in one instance was the "sponsor shock" provoked by the refugees (who had embarked from Hong Kong) carrying an electric rice-cooker, a short-wave radio, and good luggage, internationally valued consumer goods that the refugees purchased after months of working in Hong Kong factories while confined in the refugee camps for shelter. Hong Kong is the only place of first asylum for the Indochinese refugees where they are allowed to work for wages in the local economy.

6. Gouldner, "The Norm of Reciprocity," 172.

7. Dr. Tran Minh Tung, "Perspectives: Vietnamese Views on Resettlement and Adjustment," in *The Indochinese Refugee Movement: The Canadian Experience,* ed. Adelman, 159–60.

8. Jeffrey D. Fisher, Arie Nadler, and Bella M. DePaulo, *New Directions in Helping* (New York: Academic Press, 1983), vol. 1, 96–97, 134.

9. Ibid., 7–12.

10. Julia Vadala Taft, David S. North, and David A. Ford, *Refugee Resettlement in the U.S.: Time for a New Focus* (Washington, D.C.: New Transcentury Foundation, 1979), chap. 6.

11. William T. Liu, *Transition to Nowhere: Vietnamese Refugees in America* (Nashville: Charter House, 1979), 125.

12. Theodore Caplow, *Two against One: Coalitions in Triads* (Englewood Cliffs, N.J.: Prentice-hall, 1968).

13. The program became less effective (sponsors said) and overloaded—perhaps the latter caused the former. Progress was too slow using their approach, and instruction not sufficiently individuated to satisfy several refugees and sponsors. A newly funded ESL program began in September 1980 offering individualized tutoring, but only one recently arrived refugee in this study was enrolled in it. Many sponsors and refugees believed that refugees gained more in the individualized tutoring sessions that they devised. These also obviated the need to drive long distances to classes. However, the volunteers who were tutoring seldom had the time to put in full or half-days so it was not realistic to postpone employment until such training was completed.

14. I am grateful to Gail Kowalski of Genesee Ecumenical Ministries (Buffalo, N.Y.), a regional sponsorship developer for Church World Service, for data on arrivals (N = 299) and departures of Indochinese refugees sponsored through C.W.S. in the Buffalo-Rochester area arriving between 1 August 1979 and 16 October 1980 by ethnicity and nation of origin, type of sponsor (group or congregation, individual, relative), and previous contacts in the area (relatives or friends of the refugees). Cross-tabulation of the percent of arrivals moving in

that period show the percent of refugees leaving the area is as great or greater among those with relatives in the area than those without relatives or friends. Similarly, the percent of those with friends in the area leaving is as great or greater in most cases than those without any contacts leaving. It may be, as Gail suggests, that had we data of types of kinship relations enabling us to discriminate the relations with kin in both areas—i.e., the original locale of settlement and the locale of migration—that a refined test of the hypothesis that attraction to kin is a primary motive for migration would confirm it. At present, all one can conclude from these limited data is that it has not been confirmed. It may be that the experience in Riverside County only suggests that refugees who wish to settle there are more likely to find sponsors for their relatives in camps or encourage them to move there to join them.

McInnis's study "Secondary Migration among the Vietnamese," based on files of 482 families who were resettled by one Volag in the Midwest between May 1975 and October 1980, also concludes: "Initial placement in areas where relatives were living did not correspond significantly with lower levels of migration. This indicates that placement near relatives does not assure that secondary migration will not occur; it may be important where relatives are in the area." See *Journal of Refugee Resettlement* 1, no. 3 (May 1981): 36–42.

15. No investigation was made of the financial cost of these sponsorships, for it was not a focus of the study. A preliminary study of active sponsors in Riverside County in March 1980 revealed tremendous variation in the per capita and total cost, which ranged from $600 to $3,200 per committee; the mode was between $1,800 and $2,400. Variations are at times associated with whether housing is contributed, the purchase or contribution of a used car, the size of the family, the use of food stamps and Medicaid, and the length of dependency before a household became self-sufficient. No single factor seemed to explain the extent of variation. Some congregations I know of have sponsored with less than $500 on hand; others refuse to sponsor before collecting several thousand dollars. The Volag per capita grant is also a source of funds that may be sufficient in itself in some instances without collections or drawing on congregational funds.

16. Ralph H. Turner, "Is There a Quest for Identity?" *Sociological Quarterly* 16 (Spring 1975): 148–61.

17. Frank M. LeBar and Adrienne Suddard, eds., *Laos: Its People, Its Economy, Its Culture* (New Haven: Hraf Press, 1960).

18. Titmuss, *The Gift Relationship*, 237–39.

Chapter 5. Conclusions and Implications

1. Festinger, *A Theory of Cognitive Dissonance*.

2. W. C. Swabey, *Ethical Theory from Hobbes to Kant* (New York: Philosophical Library, 1961), 99.

3. Aage Bertelsen, *October '43*, trans. Milly Lindholm (New York: Gross, n.d.), 162–64.

4. Aronfreed, "The Socialization of Altruistic and Sympathetic Behavior," 105.

5. L. A. Selby-Bigge, ed., *British Moralists*, vol. 1 (New York: Dover Books, 1965), 323–24.

6. Staff members of all the congregationally based Volags told me that congregations (other than the Hispanic ones) refused to sponsor the Cubans, regardless of how much effort sponsorship developers had put in. The Volags had to rely exclusively on ethnic associations, friends, and relatives of the refugees in camps. Many of the latter turned out to be "phantom sponsors," signing papers as a service to get people out with no intention of becoming responsible for them. The rate of desertion was related by Volag representatives to the urgent need to get the Cubans out of the camps and the hasty processing of sponsors (*New York*

Times, 26 Nov. 1980). Charles Steinberg, director of the International Rescue Committee, attributed the rate of desertion to the fact that Congress had not granted them the same welfare benefits to which Indochinese and other political refugees admitted regularly were entitled. There is no comparable data on abandonment of Vietnamese refugees by individuals (friends, relatives, and private American citizens) sponsoring them.

7. The Riverside County refugee use of assistance is estimated to be one-fourth of that of all refugees in the state in which it was located on 1 August 1980. There are great disparities among states in refugee use of cash assistance, but the increase in such use continues. One may infer from estimates of population and assistance figures in 1980 that on 1 August 1980 over 60 percent of the Indochinese refugees in five states received cash assistance; similarly, the National Governors' Association and National Association of Counties reported that in January and February of 1981, 64.8 percent of the refugees in eleven states were receiving cash assistance. (For sources on the former figure, see U.S. Department of Health and Human Services Office of Refugee Resettlement, *Report to the Congress: Refugee Resettlement Program, Jan. 31, 1981:* 9, 29, and 30; and for the latter, see *Refugee Reports*, 29 May 1981.) Recent refugees (around two-thirds of whom were reportedly obtaining cash assistance) were more than twice as likely to apply for cash assistance as refugees arriving before August 1979 (*Refugee Reports*, 4 Sept. 1981, 4). Complaints about the extent of public dependency of refugees and especially of secondary migrants were regularly voiced by national and state officials in 1981. See also *Refugee Reports*, 30 July 1982, which cited O.R.R. estimates that 67 percent of all refugees in nine selected states received cash assistance.

While comprehensive records are lacking, there appeared to be an increasing use of cash assistance by refugees in Riverside County in the latter half of 1981 and 1982, but such use would probably still be substantively below that of refugees in other parts of the United States. This increase may be attributable to the recession, which affected both jobs available for refugees and the ability and willingness of congregants to give.

8. Church World Service, *Making It On Their Own: From Refugee Sponsorship to Self-Sufficiency* (New York: Church World Service Immigration and Refugee Program [mimeo.], n.d. [1984]), 16, 45, 54; U.S. Department of Health and Human Services, *Report to the Congress, January 31, 1984; Refugee Resettlement Program* (Washington, D.C.: U.S.G.P.O., 1984), 104.

9. Daniel Montero, *Vietnamese Americans: Patterns of Resettlement and Socio-Economic Adaptation in the U.S.* (Boulder, Colo.: Westview Press, 1979), 157; David S. North, Lawrence S. Lewin, and Jennifer R. Wagner, *Kaleidoscope: The Resettlement of Refugees in the U.S. by the Voluntary Agencies* (New Transcentury Foundation mimeo, February 1982), 122; U.S. General Accounting Office, *Report by the U.S. General Accounting Office: Greater Emphasis on Early Employment and Better Monitoring Needed in Indochinese Refugee Resettlement Program* (Washington, D.C.: U.S.G.P.O., 1983), 18.

10. North, Lewin, and Wagner, *Kaleidoscope*, 135–39.

11. Gail Kelly, *From Vietnam to America: A Chronicle of the Vietnamese Immigration to the United States* (Boulder, Colo.: Westview Press, 1977), 185.

12. Gertrud Neuwirth and Lynn Clark, "Indochinese Refugees in Canada: Sponsorship and Adjustment," *International Migration Review* 15, no. 1 (Spring–Summer 1981): 136.

13. U.S.H.H.S., *Report to Congress, Jan. 31, 1984: Refugee Resettlement Program*, 105; Christine R. Finnan, "Community Influences on the Occupational Adaptation of Vietnamese Refugees," *Anthropological Quarterly* 55, no. 3 (Fall 1982): 146–60.

14. Church World Service, *Making It On Their Own*, 19, concludes that: "In terms of the type of employment upgrading needed, both sponsors (49 percent) and refugees (54 percent) believe that improvement in English is the principal need, although specific vocational training is also frequently cited (39 percent and 51 percent, respectively)."

15. Joseph Westermeyer, John Neider, and Vang Tou Fou, "Acculturation and Mental Health: A Study of Hmong Refugees at 1.5 and 3.5 Years Postmigration," *Social Science and Medicine* 18, no. 1 (1984): 87–93; Perry M. Nicassio, "Psychosocial Correlates of Alienation: Study of a Sample of Indochinese Refugees," *Journal of Cross-Cultural Psychology* 14, no. 3 (September 1983): 337–51.

16. Paul J. Strand, "Employment Predictors among Indochinese Refugees," *International Migration Review* 18, no. 1 (Spring 1984): 50–64; Church World Service, *Making It On Their Own*, 27, 31. Strand's study based on 800 heads of Indochinese households in the San Diego labor market, showed that English-language communication skill is the major factor in refugee employment, while the C.W.S. study, based on 4,533 cases around the country, found that "by far the most important factor statistically is owning a car" but the "next most important factor is the principal applicant's English language fluency." The differences between the two studies may reflect the greater employer discrimination among refugees in a refugee-impacted labor market and the greater need for one's own transportation in nonurban areas. The principal difference in employment status in the C.W.S. study was between those refugees who could communicate (in English) and those who assessed their ability as "very little"; only about two out of five of the latter were employed full-time compared to three out of five of the former—rather than between those who "can communicate" and are "fluent."

17. Select Commission on Immigration and Refugee Policy, *U.S. Immigration and the National Interest: The Final Report and Recommendations of the Select Commission on Immigration and Refugee Policy with Supplemental Views by Commissioners*, 1 March 1981 (Washington, D.C.: U.S.G.P.O., 1981), 191–92.

18. Church World Service, *Making It On Their Own*, 23.

19. Neuwirth and Clark, "Indochinese Refugees in Canada," 135, remark that:

> Nearly all the refugees compared the allowance and other kinds of assistance they received from their sponsors with other refugees—indeed this seemed to be a frequent topic of conversation among refugees attending language classes. Although quite a few of them admitted that they were getting less than others they knew or had heard of, they were not necessarily dissatisfied and often stress that their sponsors were not very affluent themselves. Several refugees also seemed to place a high value on the kindness of, and social contact with, sponsors who, in their opinion, compensated for the comparatively lower level of material assistance they received. One respondent, however, remarked: "We wish all the sponsoring groups would get together and agree on the same amount. That would prevent ill-feeling among the refugees." It is also worth noting that the dissatisfaction which the few refugees expressed was not necessarily related to the actual amount received but, not surprisingly, to their previous social status in Vietnam.

20. Montero, *Vietnamese Americans*, 61.

21. Court Robinson, *Special Report: Physical and Emotional Health Care Needs of Indochinese Refugees* (Washington, D.C.: Indochina Refugee Action Center, 1980), 31–33.

22. B. Chan-Kwok and Lawrence Lam, "Resettlement of Vietnamese-Chinese Refugees in Montreal, Canada: Some Socio-Psychological Problems and Dilemmas," *Canadian Ethnic Studies* 15, no. 1 (1983): 1–17; see also reports of the prevalence of posttraumatic stress and levels of psychological distress among Indochinese refugees in *Refugee Reports*, 11 February 1983, 1, and 21 June 1985, 1.

23. Paul D. Starr and Alden E. Roberts, "Community Structure and Vietnamese Refugee Adaptation: The Significance of Context," *International Migration Review* 16, no. 3 (Fall 1982): 595–618.

24. North, Lewin, and Wagner, *Kaleidoscope*, 88.

25. The government of Canada initially pledged in July 1979 to match private sponsorships with public sponsorships in order to enable 50,000 Indochinese refugees to enter Canada. When it appeared that private sponsorships would exceed 25,000, the government altered its commitment to equal matching in order to retain the 50,000 limit, thus using private

voluntary sponsorships in lieu of public sponsorships. See discussion by government ministers, members of Parliament, and refugee advocates in Adelman, ed., *The Indochinese Refugee Movement,* 3–27.

26. Neuwirth and Clark, "Indochinese Refugees in Canada," 134.

27. Ibid., 133.

28. Victor H. Palmieri, "The Refugees: What Infighting?" *The Public Interest,* Summer 1982, 90; and Amitai Etzioni, "Refugee Resettlement: The Infighting in Washington," *The Public Interest,* Fall 1981, 15–29.

29. American Friends Service Committee et al., *Seeking Safe Haven: A Congregational Guide to Helping Central American Refugees in the United States* (New York: American Friends Service Committee, 1982), 5–6, 63–70.

30. *U.S. Immigration Policy and the National Interest,* 184–85.

31. See evaluations of planned resettlement in Arizona and North Carolina reported on in *Refugee Reports,* 2 Nov. 1984; in Idaho and Iowa in U.S.H.H.S., *Report to the Congress, Jan. 31, 1984, Refugee Resettlement Program,* C-19–C-20; and of Grand Rapids by Rev. Howard Schipper, "Indochinese Refugees Community Resources Task Force and the Problem of Assimilation" (Grand Rapids, Mich.: Freedom Flight Task Force, mimeograph, n.d.).

32. Kathleen McInnis, "Secondary Migration among the Indochinese," *Journal of Refugee Resettlement* 1, no. 3 (May 1981): 36–42.

33. North, Lewin, and Wagner, *Kaleidoscope,* 75; Neuwirth and Clarke, "Indochinese Refugees in Canada," 135.

34. Palmieri, "The Refugees."

35. Titmuss, *The Gift Relationship,* 239.

36. Ibid., 242.

Bibliography

Adelman, Howard. "Changes in Policy" and "Understanding Backlash." In *The Indochinese Refugee Movement: The Canadian Experience,* edited by Howard Adelman, 23–27, 98–110. Toronto: Operation Lifeline, 1980.

American Friends Service Committee, et al. *Seeking Safe Haven: A Congregational Guide to Helping Central American Refugees in the United States.* New York: American Friends Service Committee et al., n.d. [ca. 1982].

Arendt, Hannah. *The Origins of Totalitarianism.* Rev. ed. New York: Harcourt, Brace and World, 1966.

Aronfreed, Justin. "The Socialization of Altruistic and Sympathetic Behavior: Some Theoretical and Experimental Analyses." In *Altruism and Helping Behavior: Social Psychological Studies of Some Antecedents and Consequences,* edited by J. Macauley and L. Berkowitz, 103–26. New York: Academic Press, 1970.

Barnes, Harry Elmer. "The Social and Political Philosophy of August Comte: Positivist Utopia and the Religion of Humanity." In *An Introduction to the History of Sociology,* edited by Harry Elmer Barnes, 81–109. Chicago: University of Chicago Press, 1948.

Berenstein, Tatiana, and Rutkowski, Adam. *Assistance to the Jews in Poland.* Translated by Edward Rothert. Warsaw: Polonia, 1963.

Bertelsen, Aage. *October '43.* Translated by Milly Lindholm. New York: Gross, n.d.

Blalock, Hubert M., Jr. *Towards a Theory of Minority-Group Relations.* New York: Capricorn, 1970.

Blau, Peter M. *Exchange and Power in Social Life.* New York: Wiley, 1964.

153

Caplow, Theodore. *Two Against One: Coalitions in Triads.* Englewood Cliffs, N.J.: Prentice-Hall, 1968.

Chan-Kwok, B., and Lawrence Lam. "Resettlement of Vietnamese-Chinese Refugees in Montreal, Canada: Some Socio-Psychological Problems and Dilemmas." *Canadian Ethnic Studies* 15, no. 1 (1983): 1–17.

Chorover, Stephen L. *From Genesis to Genocide: The Meaning of Human Nature and the Power of Behavior Control.* Cambridge: M.I.T. Press, 1979.

Church World Service. *Making It On Their Own: From Refugee Sponsorship to Self-Sufficiency.* New York: Church World Service Immigration and Refugee Program (mimeo), n.d. [1984].

Collard, David. *Altruism and Economics: A Study of Non-Selfish Economics.* New York: Oxford University Press, 1978.

Dawkins, Richard. *The Selfish Gene.* New York: Oxford University Press, 1976.

Durkheim, Émile. *Suicide: A Study in Sociology* 1897. Translated by J. A. Spaulding and George Simpson. New York: Free Press, 1951.

Etzioni, Amitai. "Refugee Resettlement: The Infighting in Washington." *Public Interest,* Fall 1981, 15–29.

Fein, Helen. *Accounting for Genocide: National Responses and Jewish Victimization during the Holocaust.* New York: The Free Press, 1979.

Feingold, Henry. *The Politics of Rescue: The Roosevelt Administration and the Holocaust, 1938–1945.* New Brunswick, N.J.: Rutgers University Press, 1970.

Festinger, L. *A Theory of Cognitive Dissonance.* Evanston, Ill.: Row, Peterson, 1957.

Finger, Seymour M., ed. *American Jewry during the Holocaust.* New York: American Jewish Commission on the Holocaust, 1984.

Finnan, Christine R. "Community Influences on the Occupational Adaptation of Vietnamese Refugees." *Anthropological Quarterly* 55, no. 3 (Fall 1982): 146–60.

Fisher, Jeffrey D., Arie Nadler, and Bella M. DePaulo. *New Directions in Helping.* Vol. 1. New York: Academic Press, 1983.

Fogelman, Evan, and Valerie Weiner. "The Few, the Brave, and the Noble." *Psychology Today,* August 1985, 161–64.

Friedman, Saul S. *No Haven for the Oppressed: United States Policy toward Jewish Refugees, 1938–1945.* Detroit: Wayne State University Press, 1973.

Gallobin, Ira. "Hospitality and Hostility: Two U.S. Policies on Immigration." Mimeographed paper submitted to Consultation on Overstayed and Undocumented Persons Sponsored by the National Council of Churches, 5 May 1978.

Gallup, George. *The Gallup Poll 1935–1971*. Vol. 3, *1959–1971*. New York: Random House, 1972.

——. *The Gallup Poll 1972–1977*. Vol. 1, *1972–1975*. Wilmington, Del.: Scholarly Resources, 1978.

——. *Public Opinion 1979*. Wilmington, Del.: Scholarly Resources, 1980.

Genizi, Haim. "American Interfaith Cooperation on Behalf of Refugees from Nazism, 1933–1945." *American Jewish History* 70, no. 3 (March 1981): 347–61.

Gilbert, Martin. *Auschwitz and the Allies*. New York: Holt, Rinehart and Winston, 1981.

Glaser, Barney G., and Anselm L. Strauss. *The Discovery of Grounded Theory: Strategies for Qualitative Research*. Chicago: Aldine, 1967.

Glock, Charles Y., Benjamin B. Ringer, and Earl R. Babbie. *To Comfort and to Challenge*. Berkeley: University of California Press, 1967.

Gould, Stephen J. *The Mismeasure of Man*. New York: Norton, 1981.

Gouldner, Alvin. "The Norm of Reciprocity: A Preliminary Statement." *American Sociological Review* 15, no. 3 (April 1960): 161–78.

Grossman, Frances G. "A Psychological Study of Gentiles Who Saved the Lives of Jews during the Holocaust." In *Toward the Understanding and Prevention of Genocide: Proceedings of the International Conference on the Holocaust and Genocide,* edited by Israel W. Charney, 202–16. Boulder, Colo.: Westview Press, 1984.

Hadaway, C. Kirk. "Changing Brands: Denominational Switching and Membership Change." In *Yearbook of American and Canadian Churches 1980,* edited by Constant Jacquet, Jr. Nashville: Abingdon Press, 1980.

Haesler, Alfred A. *The Lifeboat is Full: Switzerland and the Refugees, 1933–1945*. Translated by Charles Lamm Markham. New York: Funk and Wagnalls, 1969.

Hallie, Philip. *Lest Innocent Blood Be Shed: The Story of the Village of Le Chambon and How Goodness Happened There*. New York: Harper and Row, 1979.

Hardin, Garrett J. *The Limits of Altruism: An Ecologist's View of Survival*. Bloomington: Indiana University Press, 1977.

Harrington, Michael. *Towards a Democratic Left: A Radical Program for a New Majority*. New York: Macmillan, 1968.

Hofstadter, Richard. *Social Darwinism in American Thought*. New York: George Braziller, 1955.

Holm, John D., and John P. Robinson. "Ideology and the American Voter." *Public Opinion Quarterly* 42, no. 2 (Summer 1978): 235–46.

Horne, Alistair. *A Savage War of Peace: Algeria 1954–1962*. New York: The Viking Press, 1977.

Interagency Task Force on Immigration Policy. *Staff Report*. Washington, D.C.: Departments of Justice, Labor, and State, March 1979.

Kelly, Gail. *From Vietnam to America: A Chronicle of the Vietnamese Immigration to the United States*. Boulder, Colo.: Westview Press, 1977.

Kropotkin, Petr. *Mutual Aid: A Factor of Evolution*. 1890–1896. Boston: Extending Horizons, 1955.

Kuper, Leo. *Genocide: Its Political Use in the Twentieth Century*. New Haven: Yale University Press, 1981.

LeBar, Frank M., and Adrienne Suddard, eds. *Laos: Its People, Its Economy, Its Culture*. New Haven: Hraf Press, 1960

Leboucher, Fernand. *Incredible Mission*. Translated by J. F. Bernard. Garden City, N.Y.: Doubleday, 1969.

Lenski, Gerhard, and Jean Lenski. *Human Societies: An Introduction to Macrosociology*. New York: McGraw-Hill, 1974.

Liu, William T. *Transition to Nowhere: Vietnamese Refugees in America*. Nashville: Charter House, 1979.

London, Perry. "The Rescuers: Motivational Hypotheses about Christians Who Saved Jews from the Nazis." In *Altruism and Helping Behavior,* edited by J. Macauley and L. Berkowitz, 241–50. New York: Academic Press, 1970.

Macauley, Jacqueline R., and Leonard Berkowitz. "Overview." In *Altruism and Helping Behavior: Social Psychological Studies of Some Antecedents and Consequences,* edited by J. Macauley and L. Berkowitz, 1–12. New York: Academic Press, 1970.

May, Judith. "The Vermont Experience: Planned Clusters in Snow Country." *Journal of Refugee Resettlement* 1, no. 3 (May 1981): 31–35.

McCarthy, John D., and Mayer N. Zald. "Resource Mobilization and Social Movements: A Partial Theory." *American Journal of Sociology* 82, no. 6 (December 1976): 1212–42.

McInnis, Kathleen. "Secondary Migration among the Indochinese." *Journal of Refugee Resettlement* 1, no. 3 (May 1981): 36–42.

Merton, Robert K. *Social Theory and Social Structure*. Rev. ed. Glencoe, Ill.: The Free Press of Glencoe, 1957.

Mittelman, James H., and Oukar S. Marwah. *Asian Alien Pariahs: A Cross-Regional Perspective*. Denver: University of Denver Studies in Race and Nations, Center on International Race Relations, 1975.

Montero, Darrel. *Vietnamese Americans: Patterns of Resettlement and Socio-Economic Adaptation in the U.S.* Boulder, Colo.: Westview Press, 1979.

Morse, Arthur D. *While Six Million Died: A Chronicle of American Apathy*. New York: Random House, 1968.

Nelson, Benjamin. *The Idea of Usury: From Tribal Brotherhood to Universal Otherhood.* 2d ed. Chicago: University of Chicago Press, 1969.

Neuwirth, Gertrud, and Lynn Clark. "Indochinese Refugees in Canada: Sponsorship and Adjustment." *International Migration Review* 15, no. 1 (Spring–Summer 1981): 131–40.

Nicassio, Perry M. "Psychosocial Correlates of Alienation: Study of a Sample of Indochinese Refugees." *Journal of Cross-Cultural Psychology* 14, no. 3 (September 1983): 337–51.

Nisbet, Robert A. *The Sociological Tradition.* New York: Basic Books, 1966.

North, David S., Lawrence S. Lewin, and Jennifer R. Wagner. *Kaleidoscope: The Resettlement of Refugees in the U.S. by the Voluntary Agencies.* Washington, D.C.: New Transcentury Foundation, 1982. Mimeographed.

Norwood, Frederick A. *Strangers and Exiles: A History of Religious Refugees.* Vol. 1. Nashville: Abingdon Press, 1969.

Olson, M., Jr. *The Logic of Collective Action.* Cambridge: Harvard University Press, 1965.

Onions, C. T., ed. *Oxford Universal Dictionary on Historical Principles.* Oxford: At the Clarendon Press, 1955.

Palmieri, Victor H. "The Refugees: What 'Infighting'?" *Public Interest,* Summer 1982, 88–90.

Parsons, Talcott, et al., eds. *Theories of Society: Foundations of Modern Sociological Theory.* Vol. 1. New York: Free Press, 1961.

Piliavin, Jane A., et al. *Emergency Intervention.* New York: Academic Press, 1981.

Proudfoot, Malcolm J. *European Refugees, 1939–1952: A Study in Forced Population Movement.* Evanston, Ill.: Northwestern University Press, 1956.

Rawls, John A. *A Theory of Justice.* Cambridge, Mass.: Belknap Press, 1971.

Refugee Reports, 1981–1985.

Riverside County (pseud.) Department of Planning. *Data Book 1974.* Riverside County, n.d.

Robinson, Court. *Special Report: Physical and Emotional Health Care Needs of Indochinese Refugees.* Washington, D.C.: Indochina Refugee Action Center, 1980.

Rosenham, David. "The Natural Socialization of Altruistic Autonomy." In *Altruism and Helping Behavior,* edited by J. Macauley and L. Berkowitz, 251–69. New York: Academic Press, 1970.

Ross, Robert W. *So It Was True: The American Protestant Press and the Nazi persecution of the Jews, 1933–1945.* Minneapolis: University of Minnesota Press, 1980.

Schipper, Rev. Howard. "Indochinese Refugees Community Resources Task Force and the Problem of Assimilation." Grand Rapids, Mich.: Freedom Flight Task Force, n.d. Mimeographed.

Schneewind, J. B. "Sociobiology, Social Policy and Nirvana." In *Sociobiology and Human Nature,* edited by Michael S. Gregory, Anita Silvers, and Diane Such. San Francisco: Jossey-Bass, 1978.

Selby-Bigge, L. A., ed. *British Moralists.* Vol. 1. New York: Dover Books, 1965.

Select Commission on Immigration and Refugee Policy. *U.S. Immigration Policy and the National Interest: The Final Report and Recommendations of the Select Commission on Immigration and Refugee Policy with Supplemental Views by Commissioners, March 1, 1981.* Washington, D.C.: U.S.G.P.O., 1981.

Shlossberg, Penina. "The Story of Naliboki." *Yalkut Moreshut* 2, no. 3 (December 1964). Hebrew text, English summary.

Silver, Jeremy A. *A History of Judaism.* Vol. 1, *From Abraham to Maimonides.* New York: Basic Books, 1963.

Smith, David Horton. "Voluntary Action and Voluntary Groups." In *Annual Review of Sociology I,* edited by Alex Inkeles, 247–70, Palo Alto, Calif.: Annual Reviews, 1975.

Sorokin, Pitirim A. *Altruistic Love: A Study of American "Good Neighbors" and Christians Saints.* 1950. New York: Kraus Reprint Co., 1969.

Stark, Rodney, et al. "Ministers as Moral Guides: The Sounds of Silence." In *Religion in Sociological Perspective: Essays in the Empirical Study of Religion,* edited by Charles Y. Glock, 163–86. Belmont, Calif.: Wadsworth Pub. Co., 1973.

Stark, Rodney, and Charles Y. Glock. *American Piety: The Nature of Religious Commitment.* Vol. 1. Berkeley: University of California Press, 1968.

Starr, Paul D., and Alden E. Roberts. "Community Structure and Vietnamese Refugee Adaptation: The Significance of Context." *International Migration Review* 16, no. 3 (Fall 1982): 595–618.

Staub, Ervin. *Positive Social Behavior and Morality.* 2 vols. New York: Academic Press, 1979.

Stember, Charles Herbert, et al. *Jews in the Mind of America.* New York: Basic Books, 1966.

Strand, Paul J. "Employment Predictors among Indochinese Refugees." *International Migration Review* 18, no. 1 (Spring 1984): 50–64.

Swabey, W. C. *Ethical Theory from Hobbes to Kant.* New York: Philosophical Library, 1961.

Taft, Julia Vadala, David S. North, and David A. Ford. *Refugee Resettlement in the U.S.: Time for a New Focus.* Washington, D.C.: New Transcentury Foundation, 1979.

Tec, Nechama. *When Light Pierced the Darkness: Christian Rescue of Jews in Nazi-Occupied Poland.* New York: Oxford University Press, 1986.

Theodorson, George A., and Achilles G. Theodorson. *A Modern Dictionary of Sociology.* New York: Thomas Y. Crowell Co., 1969.

Thomas, Gordon. *Voyage of the Damned.* New York: Stein and Day, 1974.

Titmuss, Richard M. *The Gift Relationship: From Human Blood to Social Policy.* New York: Pantheon Books, 1971.

Tung, Dr. Tran Minh. "Perspectives: Vietnamese Views on Resettlement and Adjustment." In *The Indochinese Refugee Movement: The Canadian Experience,* edited by Howard Adelman, 156–62. Toronto: Operation Lifeline, 1980.

Turner, Ralph H. "Is There a Quest for Identity?" *Sociological Quarterly* 16, no. 2 (Spring 1975): 148–61.

United Nations. *Human Rights: A Compilation of International Instruments of the United Nations.* New York: United Nations, 1973.

U.S. Committee for Refugees. *1980 World Refugee Survey.* New York: U.S. Committee for Refugees, 1981.

U.S. Department of Health and Human Services, Office of Refugee Resettlement. *Report to the Congress, January 31, 1984: Refugee Resettlement Program.* Washington, D.C.: U.S.D.H.H.S., 1984.

———. *Report to the Congress, Refugee Resettlement Program, Jan. 31, 1981.* Washington, D.C.: U.S.D.H.H.S., 1981.

U.S. Department of Labor. *Employment and Earnings, April 1981.* Washington, D.C.: U.S.D.L., April 1981.

United States General Accounting Office. *Report by the U.S. General Accounting Office: Greater Emphasis on Early Employment and Better Monitoring Needed in Indochinese Refugee Resettlement Program.* Washington, D.C.: U.S.G.A.O., 1 March 1983.

Van Esterik, Penny. "In-Home Sponsorship for Southeast Asian Refugees." *Journal of Refugee Resettlement,* 1, no. 2 (March 1981): 18–26.

Verba, Sidney, Norman H. Nie, and Jae-On Kim. *Participation and Political Equality: A Seven-Nation Comparison.* New York: Cambridge University Press, 1978.

Wain, Barry. *The Refused: The Agony of the Indochina Refugees.* New York: Simon and Schuster, 1981.

Ward, Lester. *Dynamic Sociology.* 2 vols. New York: Appleton, 1883.

Wasserstein, Bernard. *Britain and the Jews of Europe 1939–1945.* Oxford: At the Clarendon Press, 1979.

Westermeyer, Joseph, John Neider, and Van Tou Fou. "Acculturation and Mental Health: A Study of Hmong Refugees at 1.5 and 3.5 Years Postmigration." *Social Science and Medicine* 18, no. 1 (1984): 87–98.

White, Helen C., et al. *Seventeenth Century Verse and Prose*. Vol. 1. New York: Macmillan, 1951.

Wilson, Edward O. *On Human Nature*. Cambridge: Harvard University Press, 1978.

Wispé, Lauren, ed. *Altruism, Sympathy and Helping.* New York: Academic Press, 1978.

Wolfinger, Raymond, and J. Rosenstohn. *Who Votes.* New Haven: Yale University Press, 1980.

Woodham-Smith, Cecil. *The Great Hunger, Ireland, 1845–1849*. New York: Harper and Row, 1962.

Wyman, David S. *The Abandonment of the Jews: America and the Holocaust 1941–1945*. New York: Pantheon Books, 1984.

———. *Paper Walls: America and the Refugee Crisis, 1938–1941*. Amherst: University of Massachusetts, 1968.

Yad Vashem. *Rescue Attempts during the Holocaust: Proceedings of the Second Yad Vashem International Historical Conference, Jerusalem, April 8–11, 1974*. Jerusalem: Yad Vashem, 1977.

Yahil, Leni. *The Rescue of Danish Jewry: Test of a Democracy.* Translated by Morris Gradel. Philadelphia: Jewish Publishing Society of America, 1969.

Index

164 CONGREGATIONAL SPONSORS OF INDOCHINESE REFUGEES

Risks in helping, 29–31, 43

Riverside County, characteristics of, 56–57, 64–65

Riverside Interfaith Council, 10, 14, 53, 57–61, 69, 75, 77, 113, 115

Roman Catholic churches, 54, 69, 71, 78

Roosevelt (U.S. president), 36, 39

Rosenham, David, 29, 67

Sanctuary movement, 13–14, 130

Singapore, 45

Smith, Adam, 117

Social Defense Movements, Holocaust, 30–31, 39–43

Sociobiology, 11, 21, 22, 24

Sorokin, Pitirim A., 28–29, 67, 77

Southeast Asian nations of first asylum, 44–46

Soviet Union, 39

Spencer, Herbert, 24

Sponsor-refugee bond, 84–85, 93–97, 103–10, 117–18, 148 n.4

Sponsors, individual, 113, 120

Sponsorship (congregational) in Riverside County: and adaptation of refugees, 101–2, 119–20; assessment of by author, 108, 118–20; assessment of rewards by sponsors, 108–11, 115–16; authorization of, 71–72; breakdowns, 55, 146 n.6; community responses to, 75, 110–11, 120–21; dependency of refugees in, 119, 150 n.7; division of labor in, 77–78, 81, 87–89, 100; endings of and departure of refugees, 103–8, 118; evaluation of costs, 72–73, 115, 108–9, 149 n.15; finances and fund-raising, 78–79; functioning of committees, 98–100; goals of, 80–83, 118–20; instigation of, 61–63; joint, 98, 111; leaders, 10, 52–53, 55, 62–72, 108–14, 127–28; minority congregations response to, 58–59, 146–47 n.10; motives for commitment, 73–75; movement of, 75; organization of, 58–80, 112–15; problems in, 87, 89, 91–98; role of clergy in, 62–63, 69, 71–72, 111, 113; social process of, 80–108; tasks of, 81–83; Volag role in, 17, 58–

63

Sponsorship in Canada, 76–77, 123, 126, 146 n.47, 151–52 n.25

Sponsorship in U.S., 49–50, 53, 60–61, 79, 118–20, 124, 126–28, 133–34, 148 n.4. *See also* Refugee adaptation in U.S.; Refugee resettlement; United States: refugee legislation and policy

Stanley, William, 13

Starr, Paul D., 124

Staub, Ervin, 25

Study sample, 54–56, 146 n.5

Sympathy. *See* Empathy

Tec, Nechama, 30

Thailand, 45

Titmuss, Richard M., 14, 23, 111, 133

Tran Minh Tung, 85

Trocmé, André, 42–43

Turner, Ralph H., 109

Unemployment, 72–73

United Nations: High Commissioner of Refugees, 33, 45, 46; Refugee Convention, 19, 34; Relief and Rehabilitation Administration, 33

United States: domestic conditions impact on refugee program, 12–13, 133; Immigration and Naturalization Services, 79–80, 130; refugee legislation and policy, 14, 19, 126, 128, 130–33; response to Indochinese refugee crisis, 46–48, 51; role of (1933–45), 37–39, 45; Select Commission on Immigration and Refugee Policy, 131; State Department, 36, 130–31; suggestions for future policy of, 131–33; and war in Indochina, 67–69

Van Esterik, Penny, 80

Victims: perception of, 13, 14, 25–26, 33, 36, 41, 47–48, 52, 112, 128–29; media focus on, 145 n.42; politics of recognition, 14, 129–30

Vietnam, 44–46, 145 n.34. *See also* Indochinese refugee crisis

Volags: in Cuban refugee resettlement, 113–14, 118–20, 149–50 n.6; in Indochinese refugee resettlement, 53, 77–79, 82, 85, 87, 95, 119–20; and public policy, 126–29